TED KENNEDY
Profile of a Survivor

TED KENNEDY,
Profile of a Survivor,

Edward M. Kennedy
After Bobby,
After Chappaquiddick,
and
After Three Years of Nixon

by William H. Honan,

QUADRANGLE BOOKS

A NEW YORK TIMES COMPANY

PICTURE CREDITS

Picture. Editor—Michael O'Keefe

Cover—Ken Regan from Camera 5

1—The New York Times (George Tames)

2–3—Bachrach from Photoreporters

4–5—Bachrach from Photoreporters; Wide World

6–7—The New York Times (George Tames) ;
Richard A. Sheinwald

8–9—The New York Times (Edward Hausner)

10–11—The New York Times (George Tames) ;
Ken Regan from Camera 5

12–13—Tim Kantor

14–15—The New York Times (George Tames) ;
Ken Regan from Camera 5

16—Steve Northrup from Camera 5

For information, address:
QUADRANGLE BOOKS, INC., 330 Madison Avenue,
New York, New York 10017.
Manufactured in the United States of America.
Published simultaneously in Canada by
NELSON, FOSTER & SCOTT, LTD., TORONTO.
Library of Congress Card Number: 71—187325
Jacket photo, Ken Regan
TEXT AND BINDING DESIGN BY BENTE HAMANN
First Printing

For Nancy,
Lewis and Fifi
and Annette

ACKNOWLEDGMENTS

If I were Frank Sullivan of *The New Yorker*, I could make something of the fact that it was Herbert Nagourney who started this book on its journey, but since in my hands the result would only be doggerel I'll just say thanks, Herb, for having believed in this project from its inception. Sydney Gruson, Roslyn Targ and Zinaida Alexi were also believers from the start and I am grateful to them as well.

Since this book is an outgrowth of a series of articles written on assignment for *The New York Times Magazine,* I am naturally indebted to a number of my colleagues in the Sunday Department of *The Times*. The list begins with Daniel Schwarz, whose gracious leadership has long been an inspiration. Others who, along with Dan Schwarz, created the assignments that sent me packing after Kennedy to Boston, Washington, Salt Lake City, and once to Bismarck, North Dakota, when the chill factor was 41 below, were Lewis Bergman, Harvey Shapiro, Gerald Walker, J. Kirk Sale and Victor Navasky. When I returned to the office after each trip with no manuscript in hand but about sixty-four notebooks so scribbled that Senator Kennedy himself once remarked that the pages looked like his hate mail, the aforementioned editors were consistently reproachful until I produced copy, and for this, too, I owe them my thanks. The manuscripts were then polished to a fare-thee-well by Sherwin D. Smith, Paul Showers, and Alvin Marlens, as well as by other unseen hands. And they were strikingly illustrated by Pierce G. Fredericks, Michael O'Keefe and Ruth Block. Mike O'Keefe, whose personal file of Kennedy pictures must rival Rose Kennedy's, also served as picture editor for this book. I would like to thank, too, the photographers who accompanied me on the trips I took with Senator Kennedy—Tim Kantor and George Tames—and whose work is included in this book.

Also helpful with the manuscripts were Sally Hammond of *The New York Post,* Eugene P. Lambinus of *Saturday Review* and Nancy Burton of the Associated Press. I also turned for counsel and assistance to my chief literary advisor, Annette Neudecker Honan. Doctors Joseph Jaffe and Ferruccio di Cori were particularly helpful in guiding my psychological gropings. Harold Callen was a source of wisdom in numerous discussions of craft. Finally, there was my old friend Jon Swan who translated some of my mandarin into clear English in the process of editing the final manuscript for this book.

Phyllis Goldblatt, my attractive secretary, was simply indispensable, providing assistance with research, correspondence, telephoning and other matters too numerous to mention. Her predecessor was Dorothy Dixon, who was also a great support.

Also deserving of a paragraph all to herself is Judy Miceli, whose nimble fingers flawlessly typed the manuscript for this book.

A great many busy people pushed aside their daily burdens in order to make time to talk with me about Senator Kennedy.

Some were hostile—like Senator James O. Eastland of Mississippi who placed his feet on his desk and moved them in such a way that no matter how I craned my neck I was never able to see his face. And some were friendly and informal, as, for example, Senator Birch Bayh of Indiana who let me accompany him to the steam room in the basement of the Senate where we peered at each other through the vapors like Virgil and Dante. All, however, were generous with their time. While all I can do here is cite their names for the record, I do so in gratitude.

First, Senator Kennedy's past and present colleagues in Congress: Senator Birch Bayh, Representative Edward P. Boland, Senator Edward W. Brooke, Senator Quentin N. Burdick, Representative John C. Culver, Representative Frank Denholm, Senator Thomas J. Dodd, Senator James O. Eastland, Senator Barry Goldwater, Representative Michael Harrington, Senator Fred R. Harris, Senator Philip A. Hart, Senator Hubert H. Humphrey, Senator Roman L. Hruska, Representative Edward I. Koch, Senator Russell B. Long, Representative Allard K. Lowenstein, Senator Mike Mansfield, Senator Eugene J. McCarthy, Senator John L. McClellan, Senator George McGovern, Senator Walter F. Mondale, Senator Frank E. Moss, Senator Gaylord Nelson, Senator Claiborne Pell, Senator Joseph Tydings and Senator John V. Tunney.

Others in public life: Governor Wendell Anderson, William Dodds, Lieutenant Governor Billy Dougherty, John W. Douglas, Charles D. Ferris, Governor William L. Guy, Richard Ista, Gorman King, Governor Richard S. Kneip, Clarence Mitchell, Lawrence F. O'Brien, James Rowe, Josiah Spaulding and Al Vack.

Some colleagues in the press: Nona Brown of the Washington Bureau of *The New York Times,* Jeremy Campbell of the Washington Bureau of the London *Daily Telegraph,* John Jay Iselin of WNET–TV, Edward Kosner of *Newsweek,* Loye Miller, Jr. of the Knight Newspaper Syndicate, Martin F. Nolan of

Acknowledgments

the Washington Bureau of *The Boston Globe* and Matthew V. Storin of *The Boston Globe.*

Some members of Senator Kennedy's staff, both past and present: David Burke, Dale DeHann, Gerry Doherty, James Flug, K. Dun Gifford, David E. Harrison, James King, Paul Kirk, Melody McElligott, Wayne Owens, Carey Parker, Jerry Tinker and Andrew Vitali.

Especially deserving of praise and thanks is Richard Drayne, Senator Kennedy's able press secretary.

And finally, a few of Senator Kennedy's friends and relations: Joseph Gargan, Richard Goodwin, Milton Gwirtzman, David Hackett, Stephen Smith and John V. Tunney.

CONTENTS

TED KENNEDY
Profile of a Survivor

PREFACE

I CALL Senator Edward M. Kennedy a survivor in the title because after studying and writing about him for *The New York Times Magazine* over the past four years the thing that intrigues and amazes me is his capacity to endure. He is, of course, the last surviving son of the late Joseph P. Kennedy, but I mean to suggest more than that by the title. In recent years, Kennedy has suffered—and recovered from—more shock, defeat, punishment, dispossession, bereavement, physical hurt, and humiliation than is inflicted on most of us in a lifetime.

The fact that he has pulled through all of this does not make him a hero—some of the pain he has experienced, after all, has been deserved. His having survived so much adversity does, however, make him a phenomenon of un-

3

usual interest, for when the minor and major calamities of his recent years are enumerated the list is awesome indeed. Starting with the disclosure in 1962 that he was suspended from Harvard for having had another student take a Spanish test for him, it continues with the assassination in 1963 of his older brother, who had become President of the United States; the nearly-fatal plane crash in 1964 in which his back was broken; the assassination of another brother, who was running for President, in 1968; the automobile accident in 1969, which caused a death and led to a scandal; and the subsequent collapse of Kennedy's position as the front runner for his party's Presidential nomination. Finally, in 1971, he was ousted as majority whip of the Senate after having served in this capacity for only a single term.

Kennedy has survived all this—not just as a man but as a politician who has been neither frightened, nor shamed, nor whipped into retirement. Indeed, he has been able to "hang in there," to use the expression called out to him on the street by his fans, so tenaciously that today he is again considered a candidate for his party's Presidential nomination.

He did not emerge unscathed, of course. The Kennedy-phobes now have plenty of ammunition to use against him. And others, including many who were sympathetic to the Senator after the deaths of his brothers, have since found his conduct at Chappaquiddick, when taken together with his behavior at Harvard, intolerable. If he should seek national office they would surely vote against him.

Kennedy has also suffered internal injuries. One young man on his Senate staff recently remarked to me: "Can you *imagine* what's been going on inside him? Can you *imag-*

ine? Some day his autopsy is going to show some scars that no one—not even *us*—realized were there." On occasion, I have witnessed the pain these slow-to-heal wounds cause him. Once was when I was strolling with Kennedy through the Public Gardens in Boston and he stopped to think aloud about withdrawing from public life. That was just after the publication of the transcript of the secret inquest into the accident at Chappaquiddick in which Judge Boyle had questioned the Senator's veracity and caused him to be branded a "liar" in newspaper headlines across the country. Kennedy has since decided to continue in public service—he has, in that sense, survived Chappaquiddick— but the agonized look on his face that day as he talked about retirement brought home to me the depth of his injury.

Yet Kennedy is tough, too. In November, 1971, for instance, when I asked him if he had been hurt personally by his defeat as majority whip, he replied: "There's something about me I had hoped you would understand. I can't be bruised. I can't be hurt anymore. After what's happened to me, things like that just don't touch me, they don't get to me." I do not conclude from this that Kennedy is simply calloused. I have also recently seen him lose control of himself when reminded of his brothers. He is still very vulnerable. He has, however, developed a perspective on life, and a remarkable resilience.

Precisely how Kennedy has managed to survive all that has befallen him is, of course, a fascinating riddle. I cannot say that I have solved it in these pages. Yet I have searched for an answer, and that investigation is a theme that recurs throughout this book.

Let me quickly add that I have not written a biography.

I say nothing about Senator Kennedy's growing up, early childhood, education and other matters which properly belong in a full account of his life. At one time, I considered writing such a book, but—in the course of conversations with my brother, who was then writing a biography of Robert Browning—decided against it on the ground that Kennedy does not yet *merit* a biography. I do not mean that as a criticism; it is simply that major accomplishment still lies before him.

What I have done in the following pages, instead, is to bring together and greatly expand three separate studies of Kennedy that were undertaken as articles for *The New York Times Magazine,* and published, respectively, in February, 1969, May, 1970, and November, 1971. In each case, I was attempting to determine how Kennedy was getting over some new catastrophe—in the first instance the assassination of Robert Kennedy, in the second the publication of the transcript of the inquest into the accident at Chappaquiddick, and in the third his defeat as majority whip and the destruction of his Presidential candidacy.

In the interest of topicality, I have arranged the pieces in the reverse of the order in which they were written. Accordingly, the book begins with the latest essay in which I report what I believe to be the commencement of the third Kennedy quest for the Presidency of the United States. I then delve back to the aftermath of Chappaquiddick, and finally to that of the assassination. Also, the articles have been substantially revised. Old material has been discarded and new material added. I should further state that this book is in no way "authorized" or "official." I have not been given access to Kennedy's private files. He has not seen or "approved" this manuscript. My personal relationship with Kennedy is friendly, but we are not friends. I frequently refer to him in the following pages as Ted, because Edward strikes me as a little stiff, and Teddy, although his family nickname, has become pejorative when used by journalists.

I FIRST met Kennedy in 1968. I am frank to say that I had a low opinion of him then—as did, I believe, the majority of the press at that time. Indeed, I looked him up expecting to write something of an exposé. The previous fall I had been visiting Washington to work on an article for *The New Yorker* (it ultimately appeared in *Esquire*) about the state of the art of oratory in the United States Senate. I had completed a number of case studies of some of the more histrionic oldtimers in the Senate (such as the late Everett Dirksen, John Pastore and Sam Ervin) and, for balance, I felt I needed something about one of the younger members. I had heard Kennedy speaking on the Senate floor and had been mainly impressed by his dramatic ability. I suspected, however, that he was merely reciting lines which he only dimly understood—lines from a script prepared for him by one of President Kennedy's stable of rhetoricians, and I thought it would be amusing to bring this ghostly business to light if it happened to be true.

I became more convinced than ever that I was on the right track when I encountered difficulty getting to see the Senator. Richard Drayne, Kennedy's press secretary, kept putting me off, making me explain time and again why *The New Yorker* was so anxious to interview *Edward* Kennedy. The more overprotective Drayne's behavior

7

grew, the more intrigued and persistent I became, until finally, one day in January, 1968, Drayne said that Kennedy would permit me to call him off the Senate floor and that he would see me for a few minutes in the Senate Reception Room.

When I met Kennedy at the appointed hour, I was practically rubbing my hands with glee, confident as I was that he would reveal some horrendous secret in the course of the interview. Yet nothing of the kind happened. Indeed, he responded to all of my questions with frankness, self-confidence and an almost scholarly appreciation of the art of oratory. No, he said, he did not use President Kennedy's speech writers; he was satisfied with his own staff. Furthermore, many of his speeches were extemporaneous, such as the one he had recently delivered assailing the Administration's policy in Vietnam. "When you fill yourself with a subject," Kennedy said, "the words are there. They come easily." He went on to say he was reading his way through the ten-volume set of David J. Brewer's *The World's Best Orations,* which John Kennedy had bought in the 1950's and which the President's widow had passed on to him, knowing of his interest in public speaking. Kennedy said that he had been fascinated to come across occasional passages in Brewer that had a familiar ring to them, at which point he would realize that his brother had cribbed something from Webster, Hayne or perhaps Wilson. Then Kennedy talked about some of the speeches and speakers he personally admired.

Next, he launched into the sort of story I have since heard him tell many times—a family anecdote in which he disarmingly pokes fun at himself. "People say I sound a lot more like President Kennedy than Bobby does," he began. "I guess that's true because once during the primaries in 1960 I got to substitute for him. At this particular time he was, as usual, wherever the main action was and I was relegated to the southern part of West Virginia outside a mine shaft, passing out campaign literature as the men came out of the mine. Suddenly, a big, long car pulled up. The driver said, 'Hey! You Ted Kennedy?' I said I was, and he said 'Get in.' So I did, and the car tore out to a little airstrip. The men in the car—I didn't know any of them—hustled me aboard a light plane and we flew to Ravenswood. Finally, when we landed these guys told me what it was all about. 'Your brother lost his voice,' one of them said.

"So I travelled with President Kennedy all the next day," he continued. "At every stop, he sat on the platform and I read his speech. I gave eight or nine speeches that day. The next morning, very, very early, I heard this banging on the door of my hotel room. It was one of those guys again. He said: 'Get dressed. He has his voice now. You're going back to the mine shaft!' "

I had been impressed before, and now I was charmed and amused. We continued to talk for about half an hour, and then we slowly walked back to his quarters in the Old Senate Office Building, chatting about the Senate, Everett Dirksen, Daniel Webster, and the war in Vietnam. Suddenly, a look of alarm came over Kennedy's face and he said, "My gosh! My wife is having her appendix out. I've got to leave." So we parted, and I never mentioned him in that tongue-in-cheek article about the long-winded orators of the Senate. He seemed much too good to make fun of.

When I returned to New York City, I explained how pleasantly surprised I had been by Kennedy to J. Kirk Sale, a *Times Magazine* editor for whom I had written a number of political profiles. Would *The Times* be interested in a piece about Kennedy, I asked. Sale said he didn't think so since William V. Shannon had written an article about him a couple of years before, but he would bring the matter up at a *Magazine* staff meeting and let me know. Evidently, the thumbs were turned down when he passed along my suggestion because on February 6th Sale wrote to me: "Sorry to say that the reaction here is against a Teddy Kennedy profile since we did him only a few years ago and he has not as rosy a reputation around here as he does with you." The *Times* editors, it seemed, had much the same view of Kennedy that I had had before my meeting with him. So I filed away in the back of my mind the idea of some day writing something about Kennedy.

But events moved rapidly. In a few weeks, Robert Kennedy announced he was running for President, and then, scarcely three months later, he was shot. As Bobby Kennedy lay dying in the Good Samaritan Hospital in Los Angeles, *The Times* had its advance obituary of *Ted* Kennedy set in type, for he had suddenly become a major figure in national politics—conceivably even his party's Presidential nominee—and information about him was at a premium. On June 21st, two weeks after Robert Kennedy's death, I received a wire from Kirk Sale: "IS IT TOO LATE TO SIGN YOU UP FOR TEDDY KENNEDY PROFILE? CAN YOU FIND OUT WHEN HE'LL SIT AND LET ME KNOW EARLY NEXT WEEK?" I called back and said I'd take the assignment. At that point, however, the last thing in the world Kennedy felt like doing was to talk to a reporter, and so, of course, he was "not available." The tables had turned.

After waiting for what I considered a respectful length

of time, I called up Dick Drayne, Kennedy's press secretary, told him about my assignment and asked for an appointment to see Kennedy. It was just like old times—Drayne started putting me off again.

A LL THROUGH the summer and fall of 1968, I got absolutely nowhere with Drayne. He kept saying that Kennedy felt too grief-stricken and dispirited to want to face the press. Kennedy had permitted one or two brief meetings with Massachusetts reporters but those interviews concerned state matters and Kennedy's duties as a Senator; he did not wish to enter into discussions with members of the national press corps.

Then, on December 30th, Kennedy suddenly announced that he had decided to run for majority whip of the Senate, and at the Democratic caucus the following Friday he was elected. By that time, Kirk Sale had left *The Times* to write a book and the "Kennedy assignment" had been passed along to his colleague Gerald Walker. Gerry called me up and said that the senior Sunday editors—Dan Schwarz, *The Times's* Sunday editor; Lewis Bergman, editor of the *Magazine;* and Harvy Shapiro, assistant editor of the *Magazine*—were now very eager to get the Kennedy story written since he seemed to be emerging from seclusion and entering a new phase in his career. Accordingly, Gerry and I hatched a plan. I was to go to Washington, start interviewing Kennedy's friends and enemies in the Senate, and let word of my activities filter back to Kennedy. Our hope was that he would then figure that since I had seen so many of his enemies he had *better* talk to me just to defend himself.

The strategy was a trick as old as the newspaper business

itself. An editor I worked for years ago had explained it to me this way: "If you want a picture of Mrs. Murphy's son, and you think she doesn't want to give it to you, don't just call up and ask. Instead, call up and say, 'Madame, our newspaper is going to press tonight with a picture of your son. Frankly, the photograph we found in our files is not very flattering. I'm calling just on the off-chance that you might have a better picture of him somewhere around the house.' Invariably, Mrs. Murphy shows up with six family albums."

Even the Kennedys fall for such ploys, I was soon to learn. After conducting interviews in Washington for about a week, I got in touch with Drayne and arranged to drop by his office for a casual visit. When I met him I told Drayne my article on Kennedy was coming along beautifully—I said I had dug up some really *fascinating* material. Then I apologized for having to rush off, but explained that I was on my way to see Senator Russell Long, the spunky Louisianan whom Kennedy had just defeated as whip, and who, it went without saying, was not exactly a Kennedy fan. No sooner were the words out of my mouth than Drayne said, "I'm really going to knock myself out to get you in to see the Boss. Call me as soon as you're finished with Long and maybe I'll have had a chance to set something up." When I called back, Drayne said, "How about tomorrow at four-thirty?" So I was in. I believe I was the first reporter for a national publication to spend any length of time with Kennedy after the assassination of his brother.

Soon after the article appeared in print, I joined the staff of *The Times*. The other pieces about Kennedy for the *Magazine* followed naturally after the first and the story of their production is routine. I might just mention in conclusion, however, that after the publication of the latest of these articles in November, 1971, Kennedy called me up and said: "O.K. You convinced me. I'm running for President!" Then he laughed because, of course, he was not serious.

Or was he?

W. H. H.
New York City
January, 1972

Part
ONE

AFTER THREE YEARS
OF NIXON

I

THE THIRD
KENNEDY QUEST
FOR THE PRESIDENCY
HAS BEGUN

A MOMENT of electric drama seems to be in store for this generation of Americans. No one can say for sure when it might occur, yet it appears to be written into the script of contemporary history as an obligatory scene—one dictated sooner or later by events of the past decade. It is the moment when Ted Kennedy appears on the television screen saying, in that flat Boston twang of his so reminiscent of the voices of the other Kennedys: *"Help me finish what my brothers began!"*

He would be, of course, announcing his candidacy for the Presidency. And that is an event that would send shivers of joy, dread, anger and ecstasy throughout the country like nothing since, well . . . like nothing since Robert Kennedy's declaration on March 16, 1968. Except that this

1 7

time feelings would run higher still. Even the Kennedy haters, and those who long ago dismissed this youngest of the Kennedy brothers as a talentless trader on family reputation, and those too, who crossed him off after Chappaquiddick, could not help but be stirred by the realization that the curtain was being raised on the final act of an incredible American epic.

Could the youngest Kennedy achieve the prize that was snatched from his brothers by murderers? Or would the American political stage once again become spattered with blood and resound with police sirens? Would he go down in ignominious defeat in a state primary election, at the nominating convention, or in a general election, and thus, once and for all, dispel the "Kennedy mystique"? Or might the final tragedy be, perhaps, that this Kennedy would make it, only to become a third-rate Chief Executive and thus cruelly demonstrate the folly of a democratic society's surrender to a subliminal yearning for royalty or leaders of mythic stature? Or would Kennedy triumph? Would he, somehow, be able to realize all the bright hopes of 1960, ushering in at last the "age of poetry and power" that Robert Frost thought he foresaw as he stood on the inaugural platform that blustery day in Washington eleven years ago?

Surely, this is the stuff of drama—not quite "Greek drama" as some have said (for no one yet has found the moral significance of the plays of Aeschylus and Sophocles in the senseless killing of the Kennedys), but it is stirring drama nonetheless. And surely, this drama is of major political importance, too, for it seems destined to be acted out at the highest level of American government, and thus may have a large effect on the history of these times.

Accordingly, when I learned in November, 1971, that Senator Kennedy was about to embark on his first avowedly "political" trip since campaigning for re-election in Massachusetts in 1970, I arranged to go along with him to discover, if I could, whether 1972 is likely to be the year in which he will utter the magic words, and also to get a sense of how the country might react in case those words should be forthcoming. Kennedy decided to take his wife, Joan, as well as three staff assistants, too, and, on some legs of the journey, we were joined by as many as 14 other members of the press. We visited five states in the West and upper Midwest in November. I watched Kennedy make more than a dozen public appearances, talked privately with him along the way (and with scores of other politicians, as well), and came back to New York convinced that, despite his repeated protestations and denials, I had witnessed the commencement of the third Kennedy quest for the Presidency of the United States.

To be sure, his is an extremely tentative kind of bid, one governed by the extraordinary intricacies of his political situation, restrained by concern for his personal safety and consideration of his family responsibilities and further held back by his serious doubt that any Democrat can defeat President Nixon this year. It is a bid, moreover, that Kennedy has—at least for the time being—the power to retract should his prospects appear poor. Yet the fact that Kennedy has made a serious thrust toward capturing his party's nomination in 1972 now seems to me beyond argument.

Before reporting the details of the Western trip, let me summarize the reasons why I consider Kennedy a candidate.

First, Kennedy *says* he is not a candidate, but he has re-

19

fused to say so in terms regarded as unequivocal by persons conversant with the language that our political institutions impose on public figures. As one pro-Kennedy politican in Utah put it to me, "Kennedy has never said to us 'Hey, get off my back. I really don't want it. Go support Muskie or McGovern.'" A number of other Democratic contenders have done just that—Senator Harold Hughes last July, Senator Birch Bayh last October and Senator Fred Harris last November—and professional politicians take *them* at their word.

Kennedy could do the same thing, if he wanted to, but instead he drops hints in his speeches which, as I shall show, seem deliberately calculated to provoke speculation that he is interested in the nomination.

Second, the five-state trip I took with Kennedy, during which he met both publicly and privately with a great number of political leaders, is itself powerful evidence that he wishes to "keep the door open," as they say. To be sure, Kennedy had an articulate rationale, or "cover story," to explain each visit, but on at least one occasion, which I will describe shortly, he "blew his cover." One former national committeeman in North Dakota put it well when he said to me wryly out of the side of his mouth, "If he isn't a candidate, why did he bring his wife way the hell up here?"

Third, a reporter has to rely on intuition and whatever insight he is able to gain into the personality of his subject, and on this count let me state that as I traveled around the country with Kennedy I picked up a variety of signals whose message was one and the same: "This man is running for President." These signals ranged from a feeling I had about a speech Kennedy delivered to a group of farmers in North Dakota, which I will describe, to the fact that on every day of the trip Kennedy wore a pair of finely-wrought gold cuff links engraved with the initials "J.F.K." Now, Kennedy has become something of a mystic lately, and wearing President Kennedy's cuff links struck me as exactly the sort of thing he would do if he were indeed testing the water for a possible plunge for the Presidency. He would wear those cuff links as a kind of talisman—for reassurance, for a feeling of family solidarity, and also, perhaps, as a way of testing himself.

Fourth, if Kennedy really wants to be elected President in 1972, the best strategy for him to adopt would be exactly the one he is now pursuing. To begin with, Kennedy is not free to enter the Presidential primaries this year like the other candidates because to do so would violate his 1970 campaign pledge to the people of Massachusetts "to serve out [his] entire six-year term." Many politicians break such promises with impunity, of course, but since Kennedy cast his last campaign for re-election as an appeal for a vote of confidence after the accident at Chappaquiddick he is honor bound to live up to his pledge. So, thanks to Chappaquiddick, no primaries. And, of course, he has repeatedly declared that he will not enter any of them, and lately signed affidavits to keep his name from appearing on state primary election ballots.

Keeping out of the primaries puts Kennedy in a situation the other candidates may well envy. To be sure, one or another of them may capture a critical number of first-ballot delegate commitments by winning a string of victories in the 23 state primaries to be held this year, but it is also possible that no one candidate can dominate this extraordinary proliferation of quirky, lopsided and minor-issue-oriented contests. Moreover, it seems possible, too, that the primaries will generate such fierce rivalries that the party bosses will be forced to select a nominee from among those who remained aloof, on the theory that only such a candidate would have a chance of uniting the party in time to do battle with the Republicans. Kennedy, of course, would be an obvious choice in such a situation, especially since he alone among the Democrats does not need the primaries to prove his vote-getting ability; his remarkable standing in the polls is proof of that.

To heighten his chances of being nominated in this way Kennedy would be obliged to continually deny that he is a candidate yet, at the same time, remain active, keep his name in the newspapers and stir up an occasional flurry of speculation that perhaps he *is* interested in a draft after all. And that is exactly what he is doing.

The beauty of this strategy from Kennedy's point of view (assuming he wants a crack at the nomination) is that it gives him the possibility of declining the nomination should he determine at the last minute that Nixon is so strong that 1972 will probably be a throwaway year for the Democrats. And that option, for a man who knows his party's nomination could be literally a death sentence, is no small thing. Of course, Kennedy might not be able to say no if the party bosses came after him at the convention in desperation but at least he would be in a better position to turn them down than almost anyone else. He could say, for example, that he does not wish to subject his family to the sort of ugliness that the discussion of Chappaquiddick might stir up, and he could express concern about his personal safety and the fulfillment of his responsibilities to his own and his brothers' children.

Should Kennedy become the nominee, these defenses would, of course, become liabilities over night. But every candidate has *some* liabilities, and, usually, ways can be found to cope with them. Thus, for all the damage Chappaquiddick may have done him, it has expanded his range of options today, and since flexibility is one of a politician's most prized resources there may be moments when Kennedy looks back on the whole tragic mess as not an unrelieved disaster.

Fifth, not only do many professional Democratic politicians around the country believe that Kennedy is a likely Presidential candidate this year, but a great many Republicans do, too. And what the latter believe should not be lightly dismissed for it may be that Republican strategists have a sharper perspective (born of self-interest) on what the Democrats will do than do the Democrats themselves prior to the time of their convention.

In this light it is significant that news about Kennedy and pictures of Kennedy, appear in *Monday,* the weekly publication of the Republican National Committee, almost as regularly as in the Senator's own newsletter addressed to his constituents in Massachusetts. One eight-page issue of *Monday* published in late 1971, for instance, devoted its lead story to a denunciation of Kennedy's position on Vietnam and illustrated other stories with two pictures and one cartoon of the Massachusetts senator. This particular issue then turned its guns on Senator Henry M. Jackson, another possible nominee for the Democrats this year—the main charge leveled against him being that he was purportedly sacrificing principle "for a possible chance to be Number 2 on a Kennedy ticket."

Because they believe that Kennedy is likely to be "the man to beat," White House strategists have been engineering blocking moves against him with almost obsessive regularity in recent months. The development of the Administration's policy on the conflict between India and Pakistan furnishes a striking case in point, and as such seems worth looking into briefly before commencing the narrative of my trip to the West with the Senator.

To begin with, as chairman of a Senate subcommittee on refugees, Kennedy has had an official concern with the situation in East Pakistan, or Bangladesh, and India. Accordingly, in March, 1971, a few days after West Pakistan troops arrived in East Pakistan and began to massacre the civilian population, driving refugees by the hundreds of thousands into India, Kennedy raised the question in the Senate of whether the United States should continue to supply arms to West Pakistan. Cutting off arms shipments would not stop the killing, Kennedy acknowledged, but at least it would express to the government of West Pakistan, and to the world, that the American people were horrified by what was taking place and wished to condemn it. The Administration kept silent, however. Indeed, licenses to export military equipment to Pakistan were not cancelled by the State Department for another nine months. President Nixon's strategy was to work behind the scenes so as not to publicly embarrass the government of West Pakistan, which he considered an important military ally on the Indian subcontinent. Kennedy's view, on the other hand, was that the United States should strive to maintain friendly relations with India, the world's largest democratically governed country, as well as with Pakistan, and that in any case no "friendly relations" should cause America to pretend not to see what Kennedy was to describe after visiting India as "the most appalling tide of human misery in modern times."

24

Shortly after his opening statement in March, Kennedy made headlines by summoning several State Department spokesmen to his subcommittee on refugees and grilling them as to why American munitions continued to be shipped to West Pakistan, and as to what, if anything, the Administration planned to do to help the refugees.

The Administration first squirmed uncomfortably in this bind for a few days, then made an effective counterpunch. The day before Kennedy was due to appear in yet another forum, testifying on the plight of the refugees before a House foreign affairs subcommittee, he was handed a letter from the State Department declaring that it had authorized "an initial contribution" of $2.5 million in food and other assistance for refugee relief in India. If it was a bit un-orthodox of the Administration to announce the imple-mentation of a sensitive policy decision by sending a letter to the leader of the opposition on the issue, it was also an effective political ploy, for although Kennedy could and did argue that the Administration "must place higher pri-ority on urgently needed emergency relief" he still had to serve as its press agent, announcing that the Nixon Ad-ministration was, at least, not doing nothing.

As the number of refugees in East Pakistan swelled into the millions, and as the spectre of famine among them be-came a reality, Kennedy continued to nag the Administra-tion to increase its meagre assistance. On June 28th, at a refugee subcommittee hearing, Kennedy made it particu-larly embarrassing for an Administration spokesman by re-minding him that President Nixon had spoken out like a true humanitarian on the needs of Biafra during the 1968 Presidential campaign, yet "we haven't had either the Sec-retary of State or the President make any public statement as to their concern" about what Kennedy then estimated to be six million refugees on the brink of starvation in India. President Nixon evidently got the message; however, he waited five weeks before speaking out, then publicly took cognizance of the "prospects of famine" in East Pakistan just five days before Kennedy and his subcommittee staff were due to arrive in India to investigate the refugee situation first hand.

A second instance of the Administration's deft timing of its activities occurred when, on the very day Kennedy and his team set foot in India, Secretary of State William Rogers bolted up to New York City to have his picture taken as he handed U Thant a check for $1 million—the first American cash contribution to finance United Nations relief work in East Pakistan. Again, on the same day Kennedy returned from India, President Nixon announced the formation of a special committee on refugees—after having made a series of midnight transatlantic telephone calls the night before to hurriedly sign up the members. And just a couple of days prior to that on which Kennedy was scheduled to open hearings on a bill he introduced in the Senate that would authorize $400 million for refugee relief in India, the President interrupted a vacation at Key Biscayne to make a statement in which, for the first time, he acknowledged that war between India and Pakistan might break out as a result of the overwhelming burden imposed by millions of Pakistani refugees on the frail economy of India. In the same statement, the President announced that he would ask the Congress for a total of $250 million for assistance to refugees in the two countries.

There is nothing new, and certainly nothing sinister, in playing the game of partisan politics in this manner. President Kennedy used the advantage of the White House to play the game superbly against his opponents, and Lyndon Johnson played it with considerable cunning against Robert Kennedy in 1967 and 1968. Indeed, one could look at the facts just set forth and conclude that the American political process was being well used in this instance, for it is usually in the best interests of the country for the various members of Congress to mobilize whatever political forces they can to press administrations into action in areas where they are inclined to hesitate. What is of special importance about the facts of the matter in the present instance, however, is that they illustrate the intensity of concern that President Nixon has lavished on Ted Kennedy's every move. Indeed, they create the distinct impression that the President's hand was forced repeatedly because he did not wish to permit an issue to be developed by a young Senator against whom he thought he just might find himself running in 1972.

II

WHAT HAS COME
OVER HIM?

WASHINGTON, D.C.—My trip out West with Kennedy in November, 1971, began when I met him in the New Senate Office Building where he had been examining William H. Rehnquist, then the more controversial of President Nixon's two nominees for the Supreme Court. Kennedy must have been counting calories because he was not the "Tubby Teddy" that *Women's Wear Daily* had lately described. He looked relatively trim and seemed in a buoyant mood. We hopped into his blue 1971 Pontiac GTO, which was parked just outside, and sped out to Washington's National Airport. Kennedy's wife, Joan, looking radiant and stylish in a black and white checked wool suit, was waiting for us in the tourist-class section of the United Air Lines 727 we were to fly to Chicago. (In

Chicago, we would pick up the rest of the entourage and then fly on to Salt Lake City for the first round of politicking.) We sat three-abreast. Joan gave her husband a back-scratch as we taxied to the runway, and they held hands throughout the takeoff.

I wanted to start the first of several interviews with Kennedy by asking, not about his possible Presidential candidacy, because I did not expect to get much out of him on that score, but about the fact that he has been sounding off in recent months with uncharacteristic shrillness—so much so that Jack Newfield, the *Village Voice* journalist, told me he now regards Kennedy as "the most liberal member of the Senate—George McGovern included," and Victor Riesel, the labor columnist who has long been a Kennedy apologist, labeled some recent Kennedy statements "political pornography." Here, for example, are just a few recent Kennedy pronouncements, along with some of the reactions they have inspired.

In Washington, Kennedy told a group of 600 wives and mothers of American P.O.W.s that their husbands and sons were "rotting" in North Vietnam because President Nixon was using them as political pawns. He said the President's trip to China was "a smoke screen" behind which the President intended to continue the war, and then suggested that if he (Kennedy) were President he would have gladly "crawled into the room" at the Paris peace talks to gain their release. Barry Goldwater promptly lambasted Kennedy's statement as "disgusting" and "an insult and disgrace." Even Hubert Humphrey piped up, saying "I don't think we, as Democrats, make any points by contesting the integrity of the President in trying to end the war by negotiation, or on the prisoner-of-war issue."

Addressing 1,200 students at the Harvard Law School Forum, Kennedy scathingly attacked the Administration on a series of counts, and then added: "Richard Nixon lives in a Skinner box"—alluding to the behavioral experiments of the Harvard psychologist, B. F. Skinner. "He responds only to rewards and punishments that his senses can appreciate. Your silence is not neutral in his environment —it counts distinctly as pleasure. And this reinforces the rewards he gets from his own narrow constituency whenever he appeals to their basest instincts and panders to their prejudices." The students cheered and applauded enthusiastically, but some prominent labor leaders were reported to consider this an invitation for further campus unrest and one even likened Kennedy's speech to a call for a Maoist-style "Cultural Revolution."

In a Senate speech, Kennedy told the British to get their troops out of Northern Ireland lest Ulster become "another Vietnam." This statement threw the British press into an uproar, moved the editorial page of *The New York Times* to declare that it "raise[d] anew serious questions about his judgment," and prompted *The Washington Evening Star* to turn on a fine literary brogue, thundering: "Senator Edward Kennedy's figurative mounting of the Bogside barricades is the least helpful contribution to Irish peace since Cromwell stormed the Drogheda." To those who argued that the withdrawal of British troops would lead to a bloodbath, Kennedy calmly replied: "They said the same thing about Cyprus and Palestine and there wasn't a bloodbath there."

In Chicago, addressing the local chapter of the Council on Foreign Relations, Kennedy said the United States should explore ways to re-establish diplomatic relations with Cuba. Chicago's Republican press thereupon branded Kennedy a Castroite, and there were some old J.F.K. supporters who intoned with quavering voices that they thought they would never hear "a Kennedy cozy up to Castro."

Shortly after President Nixon sent his list of six possible Supreme Court nominees to the American Bar Association for consideration in October, 1971 (all of whom were speedily rejected) Kennedy let loose with the most blistering attack of any member of Congress. "Surely," he said, "the compilation and submission of this list will rank as one of the greatest insults to the Supreme Court in its history." A White House spokesman replied that Kennedy was having "childish tantrums."

Occasionally, Kennedy lashed out with statements so fast they ran afoul of one another. Just after the President announced his intention to visit Peking, Kennedy smothered him with praise in a Senate speech, saying: "Rarely, I think, has the action of any President so captured the imagination and support of the American people as President Nixon's magnificent gesture last week . . ." A short while later, however, Kennedy became the first member of Congress to question Nixon's good faith in making a trip to China, demanding to know whether the trip "is to be a fixed star on the road to peace instead of a passing comet in an American election year."

From New Delhi, Kennedy pronounced West Pakistan guilty of "genocide," and when he defended his national health insurance program (a plan that, if adopted by Congress, would be the most revolutionary piece of legislation to come out of Washington since Social Security) he blasted not only the A.M.A. but the Blue Cross Associa-

3 1

tion, too, accusing the latter of using the premiums paid by its subscribers to finance a Washington lobby opposed to his program.

What on earth, I had been wondering, has happened to the temperate, guarded, endlessly diplomatic Kennedy who, for example, back in 1969 had agonized for three weeks, changing his mind almost every day, over the question of whether or not to write a preface for a collection of scholarly "white papers" opposing the further installation of ABMs. Kennedy had been a leader of the Senate fight against the ABM at that time, but suddenly he began to fear that compiling a book of essays on the subject by a bunch of Harvard professors might make him appear "too aggressive." Would this book offend the patriarchs of the Senate? In what size print should his name appear on the cover? Was the title overly sensational? Was the jacket design too flashy? Finally, the book came out with Kennedy's name on the preface, but he nearly drove his associates up the wall before he made up his mind. And that was characteristic of the way Kennedy operated in those days.

So what had come over him?

SOMEWHERE OVER THE MIDWEST—I began our conversation on the plane by asking if Kennedy was enjoying political life these days.

"Yes, very definitely," he said. "It's probably a result of a number of different circumstances. Now that I'm no longer assistant majority leader (Kennedy was defeated seeking re-election as majority whip of the Senate in January, 1971), I have more time, more flexibility. Just physically, it's freed me up. Also, as we come into a national campaign year, there's a sharper public interest and attentiveness. More people are listening. There's a climate which is conducive from both the listener's and the speaker's point of view. Another thing is that it seems to me that the time has come for some of the issues that I've been interested in for a long while. Refugees, for example. I've been concerned with the refugee problems around the world since 1965, but now that we have this situation in India and Pakistan the public's caught up, maybe. So when I speak about that, people respond. I've been talking about Communist China since 1967, and now they're in the United Nations and so that issue has come alive also. Then, I've progressed myself. I became chairman of the health subcommittee last year, so I can do more about that."

Did he think he had moved politically to the left in recent months? "Well, it's difficult in terms of my own critical judgment to feel any change. I feel, at any given time, I'm doing what needs to be done, what's right. I know there are areas that my brother Bob was interested in—more interested than I at the time—and I suppose I have moved into some of those areas to carry on. But I don't know that that's taken me to the left. You see, in terms of our general philosophy, my brother and I started off the same. Much of the input from the family was the same. Our exposure and development as human beings was very similar. And so we moved in similar, or maybe parallel, directions. Bob was interested in education; I got interested in health. He got involved in the problems of the Middle East; I spent more time on the problems of the Far East. But we had the same general parameters of interest and concern."

"If you haven't actually moved left," I said, "you do

seem more liberated now. You know how we always used to write those 'Good Senator Kennedy' articles about you because you were so deferential to the patriarchs, almost slavishly attentive to the courtesies—like not speaking out on some issue that a senior member might have staked out for himself, and that sort of thing."

"And now you don't write those articles any more," he said, laughing.

"Right, because since losing the whip fight in January, you've changed, haven't you?" (What I was getting at is that I suspected the whip fight had taught Kennedy that since his ascension as a national figure in his own right after the death of Robert Kennedy, there was little profit for him in playing by the "rules" of the Senate "Club," or ruling clique. He failed to be re-elected whip because a number of senators simply flouted the unwritten rules that he himself had always religiously adhered to. On the eve of the election, 28 Senators, or exactly the number necessary for his re-election, gave Kennedy personal assurances they would vote for him, but when the ballots were counted he had only 24 votes, and lost. Curious Washington reporters then asked each Democratic Senator how he voted and 26 claimed they had voted for Kennedy. Thus, at least a few Senators had lied twice—once to Kennedy and once again to the press—demonstrating to Kennedy in the most personal way that no matter how exemplary a by-the-rules player he himself might be, he could no longer expect reciprocal treatment. He had become a major national figure, and, in the process, lost the immunities which an otherwise circumspect and winningly mannered young Senator might enjoy. At the same time, I guessed, Kennedy thereafter felt less held in check by the fear of stepping on toes

and was free to do some of the things he had long wanted
to do.)

"I think that's partially true, yes," Kennedy began.
"Along the road there have been some things that made a
dramatic impression on me. Losing the whip fight, yes, that
was one of them. But I don't take it too hard. One can't
afford to be spiteful in politics."

But had losing the whip fight taught him a lesson—that
playing by the rules isn't going to keep his colleagues from
taking advantage of him when they get the chance?

He laughed, then said, "Well, that drove it home, yes!"

Was the lesson especially well learned because it hurt
personally?

"Look," he said, changing his mood abruptly. "There's
something about me I had hoped you would understand. I
can't be bruised. I can't be hurt anymore. After what's
happened to me, things like that just don't touch me, they
don't get to me. I sincerely don't feel embittered. I learned
something about the Senate, yes, but that's as far as it goes."

But what he had learned about the Senate resulted in his
speaking out more freely, had it not?

"Yes, very definitely."

Was another factor in his recent liberation a degree of
fatalism resulting, perhaps, from the deaths of his brothers?

"That's fair enough, yes."

Was he a fatalist?

"No. Not really. But I suppose, well, the small things
don't matter as much. I have more perspective on what is
and what is not important."

And taking himself out of the Presidential race, after
Chappaquiddick, had that freed him also?

"Yes. I guess so."

"What is the purpose of this trip?" I asked.

Kennedy replied: "Wayne Owens was my assistant in the whip's office and he ran Bob's campaign in the Rocky Mountains area in 1968. Wayne always said he wanted to go back to Utah and run for office and so when he did go back he asked if I'd come out and speak for him. I said fine. The same sort of thing developed in South Dakota with Billy Dougherty—he ran Bob's campaign there in 1968 and now he's running himself and needs help and so I said I would go up there, too.

"Then when the invitation came in from the National Legal Aid and Defender Association through John Douglas —he's an old friend and that's a cause I've long been interested in—I put those other two sort of back to back. Walter Mondale is one of the people in the Senate I have the most respect for and so when he asked me to stop off in St. Paul on the way home I added that one."

But didn't his taking a trip around the country like this, speaking on all these occasions, suggest that he was running for something?

"The end of that sentence could be that it proves I'm *not* a candidate. *I'm* speaking out. The ones who *are* candidates are not. If you're interested in what's going on, you don't want to keep silent. Also, by speaking out on controversial issues, you're likely to have a diminishing standing in the polls. I see a good possibility of that happening to me."

When he made the statement last August that he would not endorse any Presidential candidate until the Democratic convention opens in July, a great many people said that meant that he himself was a candidate. What about that?

"I think there are two ways you can be effective. If you

endorse a candidate, then you ought to go to Peoria and Evansville and all the rest and speak for him. The other way is to stay on the floor of the Senate, speaking out and attempting to move the party and get Congressmen and Senators to take positions. I've selected the second way. Besides, if you endorse someone you're just as liable to speculation."

Was he certain he would not enter any of the primaries?

Kennedy turned and looked me in the eye. "I won't. I've said I won't. I just won't do it."

What if no one emerges a clear victor from the primaries, and his party turns to him and says it needs him to unite it? And suppose the polls show he's the only one who can do it. Wouldn't he feel a *responsibility* to run?

"No," he said, shaking his head. "I have other responsibilities which have the highest priority. I don't think I have to make a choice which is going to subject my family to concerns which I feel they ought not be subjected to."

"But the pressure can be enormous," I replied. "Look at 1952. At first, there were all those people in the primaries —Alben Barkley, Richard Russell, Averell Harriman, Robert Kerr, Estes Kefauver—cutting each other up and getting nowhere. Adlai Stevenson didn't want any part of it and kept saying no because he didn't think he could beat a victorious general, but then the convention turned to him in desperation and he couldn't resist the pressures. He couldn't resist them again in 1960. He didn't want to run then either, but got sucked into appearing on the convention floor where he looked very silly. What makes you think you can resist those pressures if the primaries in 1972 are inconclusive?"

"It didn't really trouble me in 1968," Kennedy answered. "There were legitimate inquiries made and potentialities explored in terms of that situation. But I said no."

"Yes," I continued. "But then you had just lost your brother and that was a special situation which everyone could understand. How could you defend yourself from those terrific pressures, if they ever get going, this time?"

"Perhaps I've been in a fortunate position in having been intimately involved in, and now have some insights into the realities of, you know, national politics. It's given me some degree of anticipation and perspective."

Did he think that someday in the future he would like to run for President?

"Well, the Presidency is the focal point. That's the place where you can accomplish the most. Some people say, 'You mean you'll never run?' Of course, I wouldn't say that. Obviously, my responsibilities in terms of family change. Children grow. Things change. But this is not a question or a problem for me to think or worry about now. It has been sharply impressed upon me not to plan for the future. I feel a sense of achievement in terms of the Senate, participating in the events and passions of our times."

Would he feel he had let his brothers down if at some point he did not at least make a try for the Presidency?

"No, I don't feel that."

If he is going to run for the Presidency, the longer he waits and the farther away in time that he gets from his brothers, the more he becomes his own man, a creature of the issues of that time instead of a creature of a dynasty from the past. Was that a consideration in his holding off for the time being?

"Naturally, as a man, you'd like to do it yourself. I'll always remember that my name is Kennedy and I'll always be proud of that, obviously, but doing it at a different time and era has its appeals."

I next turned to the problem of Kennedy's personal security. It was difficult to ask a man in front of his wife if he thought he might get shot, but the subject had to be faced. Criminologists and law enforcement officials believe that Kennedy's life is in some degree of danger today because of what is called the "symmetry proposition"—that is, the compulsion of psychotic persons to commit acts, often criminal acts, that will complete cycles or fill out patterns. Killing the last of the Kennedy brothers would be such an act.

This danger to Kennedy is believed to be compounded whenever he makes controversial public statements. For example, when Kennedy made a strong statement about Vietnam a short while ago his hate mail rose in volume, whereas when he was defeated as whip in January, 1971 it slackened. If Kennedy were to become a declared candidate for President, it seems reasonable to assume, he would be in maximum danger not only because he would then be making controversial statements that would receive the widest possible publicity but also because he would be adding another element to the symmetry proposition—becoming the third brother to associate himself with the office of the President.

Even now, Kennedy receives more threats on his life than anyone else in the country except the President. According to one count made last February, between the time of the assassination of President Kennedy and 1971, Kennedy received 355 threats serious enough to be investigated by the Secret Service. (The next two most-threatened Senators were Eugene McCarthy and Barry Goldwater, who received 99 and 94 threats, respectively, during the same period.) Kennedy is now receiving about two death threats per week. The Secret Service does not have the authority to protect members of Congress, but traditionally it has investigated threats to all public officials on the ground that persons making such threats are a potential danger to the President and the Vice President. Would-be assassins, of course, do not customarily write letters or make phone calls to warn their intended victims, but threats and hate mail, as one Kennedy staff man expressed it to me recently, "show where you are on the love-hate scale in the country." He added, ominously, "And you never know when that hate is getting through to some guy lying in a rooming house somewhere."

The question of Kennedy's personal security is important also because it may actually constitute a political liability for him today. A pro-Kennedy union leader I spoke to in Washington told me he happened to be present at a small gathering of politically prominent Democrats one evening in September, 1971 when a couple members of the group said they were interested in starting a draft-Kennedy movement. Another member of the group (pledged to another candidate) skillfully exploited the security question to quash the draft-Kennedy proposal. "This guy said we shouldn't take it upon ourselves to risk putting a family through that ordeal three times," the union man said, continuing: "People really wanted to come out for Ted, but this guy kept saying 'Don't do him that favor.' There were a couple of women present, and he really got to them. They haven't come out for Kennedy yet. This is the kind of argument against the Senator that no one would say publicly, but it could be used at night meetings, and that sort of thing."

Of course, if the question of Kennedy's personal security ever became an open political issue, even a subterranean one such as this union man suggested, it might well backfire, much like the question of Eisenhower's heart condition in the campaign of 1956. In any case, since this matter is of critical importance, I asked Kennedy if the question of his personal security was keeping him from running for President.

He started to drum his fingers on the arm rest as he answered. His wife was rigidly attentive and silent. "I would say," he began, "that my decision on this matter is made in terms of fulfilling family responsibility to my own children and my brothers' children, my wife and mother and sisters. I have to look at my interest in public affairs in ways that are consistent with their welfare, not for my own but for their peace of mind, and within that framework the security question raises itself."

"A member of your family told me," I said, "that your running for President in 1972 would be like leaving money on the bureau—it's unfair to the maid. Your running for President, this member of your family said, would be an unfair temptation to all the disturbed people in this country. Do you look at it that way?"

"No, I don't," he answered coolly. "If you took it lightly and said there was nothing to it, you'd be a fool. On the other hand, if you worried about it all the time, you'd be valueless. So you have to bring these two things into balance and make an evaluation. And you have to think of what this means in terms of the other people in your life."

"Has anyone ever made an attempt on your life?" I asked.

"No. Never," he said. "I guess there was one situation in which someone called the office and said his roommate was very disturbed and had a gun and was coming to Washington on a bus. He said he was due to arrive at a certain time. I was informed. The situation was taken care of."

"Sometimes," I said, "I think maybe you'd like to lower your head, run for President, get it all over with and then go back to leading a normal life. Do you ever think of that?"

"No," Kennedy answered. "I really enjoy my work. Obviously there are times of disappointment and frustration. But basically I enjoy the challenge and the opportunity of what I'm doing now in the Senate."

Before turning from the matter of Kennedy's security, I might mention here an experience which, though it occurred later in the course of this trip, is illustrative of the precautions taken by local police throughout the country when Kennedy comes to town. After one of Kennedy's appearances, I became separated from him in a crowd and finally caught up with the Senator just in time to see him climb into his car, close the door and pull away. I ran to a car directly behind his, received a nod from the driver and jumped in the back seat. As we followed Kennedy's car to our next stop, the driver and the man sitting beside him told me they were among the members of the plainclothes security division of the local police force assigned to protect Kennedy as long as he was in their city. I asked why they let a stranger like me practically dive into the back seat of their car. One of the men turned around and said with a smile: "Because we know who you are. You're staying in Room 1322 of the Hilton Hotel. You ordered a bottle of Heineken's when you arrived and you've been complaining to the management that a typewriter was not delivered to your room." I had to congratulate them.

A minute or two later, a cream-colored convertible passed the car we were riding in, and proceeded to pass Kennedy's car, too. The plainclothesman beside the driver broke off the conversation, slipped his hand inside the front of his jacket and held something there until the convertible was out of sight.

III

NIXON'S
'FORGOTTEN PROMISES'
AND KENNEDY'S
FUTURE PROMISE

SALT LAKE CITY, UTAH—Swarming around our airplane when we stepped out were enough reporters with microphones, cameras, flash bulbs, klieg lights and TV cameras to make me think for a moment we must have broken some sort of speed record on the way out. A collection of the state's leading Democrats was there, too—with the notable exception of Governor Calvin Rampton, who was soon to declare for Senator Edmund Muskie—and their presence was expressive of the fact that Kennedy has some remarkably solid organizational backing in Utah. I later learned, for example, that he had recently received *written* statements begging him to run for President from three of the top Democrats in Utah, as well as from a host of lesser party officials and supporters.

44

After a quick press conference (at which Kennedy declared he was not a candidate), and the traditional visiting politician's audience with Joseph Fielding Smith, the 95-year-old leader of the Church of Jesus Christ of Latter-day Saints, Kennedy attended a $25-a-plate roast beef dinner for his friend Wayne Owens in the barn-sized Hotel Utah. At first, it seemed a legitimate enough thing for a non-candidate to do—Owens had run the whip's office for the Senator—but I later discovered that it was what Owens had done for his brother Robert that really endeared this man to Edward Kennedy.

Shortly after Bobby entered the Presidential race in 1968, Owens staged an enormous gathering at the Terrace, one of Salt Lake City's largest ballrooms, at which Bobby was invited to speak. Just before Bobby left his hotel room for the Terrace, however, the police notified him that there had been a bomb threat. Bobby and Owens went over to have a look and found about 4,000 people milling on the street outside, and they assumed the police had emptied the hall. They soon learned, however, that this huge crowd was only the overflow; another 6,000 were jammed *inside* the ballroom, and this latter group had refused to leave their seats even after the police announced that a bomb threat had been made, and that the hall could not be thoroughly searched unless it was emptied. So Bobby sauntered in, made a quip about starting off the evening with a bang and enjoyed one of the most memorable triumphs of his Presidential campaign.

Kennedys don't forget, and so, as Ted Kennedy said in his after dinner speech, he had come back to Salt Lake City to thank everyone because "you gave my brother one of the finest receptions he ever had," and to thank Wayne Owens

4 5

for his "energy and inspiration . . . and the priceless quality of judgment he brought to all our councils."

The Senator then launched into a speech I had heard him deliver on two previous occasions in New York City and which I was to hear him recite a number of times during this trip to the West. The reporters in the entourage dubbed it the "forgotten promises" speech because in it Kennedy listed five promises which, he said, Richard Nixon had made to the American people in 1968 and since failed to keep. The speech is worth including here in some detail because it will probably serve as Kennedy's basic speech for 1972. In all likelihood he will continue to deliver it right up to the time of the Democratic nominating convention in July, modifying it when necessary and departing from it altogether on special occasions but relying on it for those day-to-day appearances in which politicians are called upon to spell out their principal differences with the opposition. Every Presidential candidate, and indeed every politician, goes into an election year with a basic speech of this sort. What is especially important about Kennedy's is that it identifies what he considers the most profitable political issues for the Democrats this year, and, should Kennedy himself become his party's nominee, the ideas and even language in this speech would surely thread their way into the Presidential campaign of 1972. One can already begin to assess their potential effectiveness.

"Not since the Great Depression forty years ago," Kennedy began, "has the spirit of America been so depressed, has there been such a sense of pessimism and defeat as now stalks the land." The chief reason Americans feel this way, he continued, is that "the promises we heard from the Republicans in 1968 lie buried and forlorn. . . . Let us look

4 6

tonight at what they promised in 1968. It was not that long ago. You can remember it as well as I." And then he took up the first of the five forgotten promises.

"The first forgotten promise, the one that leads all the rest is the promise on the war. Mr. Nixon told us in 1968 that he had a plan to end the war and lead us to a generation of peace.

"The American people believed him. They voted overwhelmingly to end the war in the primaries of 1968. They voted overwhelmingly to end the war in November, 1968. And yet, since then, there hasn't been a single week, a single month, when American men have not died in battle in Vietnam.

"Yet, week after week, month after month, a clear peace offer lies unanswered on the conference table in Paris. The President is off for talks in Peking, and on to Moscow, in search of peace, but why doesn't he do something about the peace talks in Paris, which began two years ago?

"I would like to hear President Nixon say, just once, that it was a mistake for America ever to get involved in Vietnam.

"Sixteen thousand Americans have died in Asia since November, 1968, and still the war goes on.

"It goes on in Laos and Cambodia. It goes on for hundreds of thousands of injured civilians.

"It goes on for millions of homeless refugees. It goes on for our prisoners and their families.

"And last October, while the war went on, America stood like a pitiful, helpless giant and watched the government of South Vietnam play out the cruel charade of their rigged referendum, instead of the free and fair election they ought to have. . . .

"We thought we had a promise, and that was 1968. The American people want the war to stop. They want our troops and prisoners to leave that tragic land today. They want them to come back home where they belong. They want to bring our boys home from Vietnam now—not on President Thieu's schedule, but now!"

Kennedy was interrupted by a good, strong round of applause at this point—a predictable response, considering that he was among friends and fellow Democrats. The fact is, however, that while Kennedy scored a good debater's point about the "rigged referendum" in Vietnam, which is and which deserves to be a source of embarrassment to the Administration, his argument that Nixon forgot his promise to end the war will look weak indeed, if, by the time of the Presidential campaign, Nixon has succeeded in "winding down the war" according to his present schedule. Kennedy knows this; in fact, he told me privately at one point later on during the trip that he has been informed that Nixon's present objective is to reduce the number of American troops in Vietnam by the summer to the number that were there during Eisenhower's last year in the White House, and then to make a big point of this equation in his campaign. If Nixon is able to accomplish this objective (and, of course, he could do it not only by bringing troops home but by moving support troops to Thailand), it will look very much as if he *has* fulfilled his promise to end the war. Besides, he may adroitly create the impression that the war was a misadventure of the Democrats which the Republicans, as soon as they returned to power, wound back down to a sensible and relatively harmless level. While the Democrats, in turn, could hammer away at Nixon's own misadventures in Laos and Cambodia, and say that he did not stop the war soon enough, such charges might sound disingenuous coming from the party that supported Lyndon Johnson and Hubert Humphrey. So the war issue does not appear likely to be a strong one for Kennedy, or any other Democrat this year. Unless, of course, there should be a sudden upsurge in military activity.

Next, Kennedy turned to the second "forgotten promise," which, he said, was the President's pledge to "end inflation." He called attention to the economic slump by touching on such unpleasant facts as the high interest rates charged in Salt Lake City and the number of jobs lost throughout Utah. (As he repeated this speech in the days ahead, of course, he would be substituting local references and unemployment figures appropriate to the other states he visited.)

"You don't have to tell the housewives of Salt Lake City about inflation," Kennedy said. "You don't have to tell the homeowners about the property tax.

"You don't have to tell the copper workers at Kennecott about layoffs and rising unemployment.

"You don't have to tell the businessmen of Utah that interest rates are out of sight. You don't have to tell anyone in this great state that President Nixon has put the economy through the wringer.

"Many of our largest enterprises now find their earnings are higher in Europe and Asia than they are in the United States. I say, it is a sad day for America when our corporations must go overseas to make a profit.

"Nearly 25,000 citizens of Utah are out of work today. Five million Americans have lost their jobs across the country. No one's job is safe as long as this Administration is in power.

"You know the way things went. They got bad in 1969. They grew worse in 1970. And now in 1971 we have the freeze and the promise of Phase II. I hope it works. I think it may. But no amount of rhetoric or organization charts in 1971 can mask the fact that they should have acted long ago, in 1969.

"And it's all because the Administration tried to use the same old formula. The same old do-nothing Republican formula that has failed so often in the past, and that is causing so much suffering now in the factories of Utah, the mills of Massachusetts, and plants throughout the nation.

"Why should the American people be surprised? That formula never worked before. It didn't work for William McKinley. It didn't work for Herbert Hoover. And it hasn't worked for Richard Nixon."

Once again, Kennedy received strong applause, yet here, too, his argument seemed as though it might look weak by the time of the Presidential campaign later this year. For the fact is that when President Nixon announced a wage-price freeze in August, 1971, and thereby committed himself to an activist approach to stimulating the nation's flagging economy, he took an issue away from the Democrats. *Variety*, the show business weekly, expressed the situation aptly when it reported the President's new tactic and the subsequent sharp upswing in the stock market in the headline: "Prez Changes Economic Game Plan: New Score is Dow Jones 32; Nixon '72."

Of course, the Democrats can argue, as Kennedy did in Salt Lake City, that Nixon failed to act soon enough— after all, the Democrats had been recommending the introduction of economic controls of one sort or another for months, even years, before Nixon took action. Yet here again, as with the war issue, the Democratic position boils down to little more than "I said it first"—in a position all too frequently occupied by political losers. Furthermore, even if the economy is not in an ebullient state of health by election time, Nixon can always say that effective preparatory measures have already been taken and that prosperity is just around the corner, if only the people be patient and re-elect the team that drew up those measures. Unless the economy really begins to collapse, the Democrats will have a tough time countering this argument.

"The third forgotten promise," Kennedy continued, "is on welfare. Mr. Nixon told us in 1968 that we could not truly help the poor until we got them off the welfare rolls and into jobs.

"But since he came to office, welfare rolls have risen by the millions. Now, we find ourselves paying welfare not just to the poor, but to tens of thousands of others—to engineers in Salt Lake City, to white collar workers throughout the state, and to all the rest who have lost their jobs through years of Republican neglect.

"Mr. Nixon has a program of welfare reform, but he let members of his own party scuttle it in Congress. I stood on the Senate floor a year ago and watched a decent welfare reform bill go down to defeat because the Republicans were against it.

"You don't have to look very far to find the reason. This Administration is much too interested in welfare for Lockheed and tax incentives for big business. . . ."

There was a polite patter of applause as Kennedy wound up his third point, but the fact that it was polite rather than enthusiastic seemed to confirm my supposition that while the public is deeply concerned about the increasing cost of welfare, the Democrats may have a difficult time making this concern pay off politically.

As Kennedy said, the Administration presented a program for welfare reform—a program so liberal, in fact, that a great many Democrats supported it. There is still a chance that the President's bill may be reported out of committee and passed into law this year. If it is not acted upon by Congress, however, the public is unlikely to perceive this as being the President's fault. I just cannot imagine that Kennedy or any Democrat will get very far by saying that Nixon "let members of his own party scuttle it in Congress." And while a Democratic candidate for President might say he would place a higher priority than the present Administration on welfare reform, who could really be sure of what that would accomplish?

"The fourth forgotten promise is on crime," Kennedy went on to say, and here at last he seemed to have an issue with high potential impact.

"Mr. Nixon told us in 1968 that he would bring us law and order. You don't have to tell the people of Utah that in the first three years of this Administration, major crimes have risen to their highest level ever, or that shootings of policemen are on the rise. You don't have to tell the people here that crime in Utah is above the national average.

"But the President has done one thing. To hide the bad results, he has begun to doctor the F.B.I. crime reports. Do you believe John Mitchell when he says we are making progress, when all he can tell us is that crime is going up, but the rate of increase is going down?

"Now, if you are sick, and your temperature rises two degrees, from 102 to 104, it is not much comfort to know that it rose three degrees the day before, from 99 to 102.

Would you believe a doctor who said you were getting better because you were getting sicker at a slower rate?" This drew laughter and applause.

"As long as crime goes up, we are failing in our effort.

"When we reach the point that even our policemen can't be safe on the streets of our major cities, then I say we need new leadership, and we need it right away."

Once again Kennedy was enthusiastically applauded. Utah, and indeed all of the Western and Midwestern states Kennedy visited on this trip, have nothing like the problem with crime that city dwellers of the East and Far West know, but according to the opinion polls people everywhere are alarmed by what they read about crime in the newspapers and hear about it on television, and so the issue appears to be a vital one. Furthermore, the progressive increase in crime, which no one seems to know how to prevent, is an issue that works against whomever is in power. Nixon used it to good effect against the Democrats in 1968; they, in turn, will quite probably win some support when they use it against him this year. This is not to say Kennedy's point here was demagogic. He was not claiming that he knew how to stop crime, only that the Administration had been kidding the public—a fair enough point to make.

"The fifth forgotten promise," Kennedy continued, "is the forgotten promise of reconciliation." And here he turned to an issue that could be enormously potent in the 1972 campaign, especially in Kennedy's hands. Internal divisiveness has reached an uncomfortably high pitch in American society today, and here again the opinion polls have revealed a widespread yearning in the electorate to see the country somehow brought together again. Richard

53

Nixon and Spiro Agnew, as a result perhaps equally of the particular charisma they project as of their policies, have widened rather than patched the cracks—and it seems improbable that they can significantly alter their behavior or achieve a markedly different result in the months ahead. While Kennedy, too, is what political scientists sometimes call a "polarizing," or potentially divisive, figure—witness, for example, the extraordinary quantity of "hate mail" and threats that he receives—he has an interesting potential as a pacifier and uniter. Being a younger brother in an intensely competitive family, he developed the temperament of a peacemaker at an early age. Furthermore, for a great many Americans Kennedy seems to symbolize a hatred of violence (he need only allude to "the events of 1968" or "the events of 1963" to remind one of that), and also the desire to restore things as they were in a happier, less bitterly divided era. (The early 1960s may have been just as beset with conflicts as the present, but to many people they seem comparatively untroubled in retrospect. Indeed, the years during which John F. Kennedy was President have been glamorized and glorified almost beyond recognition—to a paradisiacal era in which even hard-bitten ward heelers supposedly went around asking not what their wards could do for them but what they could do for their wards. Kennedy does not encourage such fantasies; he simply cannot avoid taking advantage of them.) Such thoughts were powerfully awakened as Kennedy spoke of the fifth and last of Nixon's "forgotten promises" and then launched into his peroration. Reading the words he spoke then, it is possible to imagine how Kennedy might capitalize very effectively indeed on this appeal which is uniquely his own in a Presidential campaign.

"Can anyone forget the bitterness of 1968, the hate and violence of that tragic year?" he said. "And can anyone forget little 13-year-old Vicki Cole, of Deshler, Ohio, the girl who held up that eloquent sign to Richard Nixon in the '68 campaign? 'Bring us together,' said the sign, and all of us had hope.

"We remember the promise by our newly-elected President on that November morning in 1968, when he quoted from the sign. He said he would bring America together, and two hundred million people said Amen.

"That promise lies broken now, broken like all the others, shattered by an Administration that has set black against white, rich against poor, old against young, business against labor, north against south. . . .

"Where is the leadership we used to have? Where is the vision and commitment that made America great? Where is the inspiration we need to meet the challenge?

"I'll tell you where they are. They are just where they have always been—in the leadership and the vision of the Democratic party. Call the roll of leading issues, and you find giants in the Democratic party at the helm:

"Men like Muskie on pollution, Humphrey on civil rights, McGovern on the war, Jackson on the Middle East, Harris on the common man, Mills on the economy, and Mayor Lindsay on the cities. . . .

"Those are the sort of men we're going to elect in 1972. We can win a great victory for America next year.

"And with the victory we win, we will have leaders who keep their promises. We will have leaders who make America strong and respected at home and overseas. We will have leaders who kindle once more our spirit of hope and confidence—a spirit that trumpets to the world that Amer-

5 5

ica is still the last great hope for peace and liberty of all mankind.

"That's the way John Kennedy put it, when he came to Utah in 1960.

" 'The point of the matter,' he said, 'is that this great country of ours deserves the best in leadership. It deserves a President who will set before our people the unfinished business of our society. It deserves a President who believes America can move ahead. . . .'

"He closed the rally that night with the line he loved from Robert Frost—'I have promises to keep, and miles to go before I sleep.'

"These words are as valid now as they were a decade ago.

"And so I ask each of you tonight to look upon the coming weeks and months as a challenge to call forth again the best in us and in America. I ask you to summon all your vision and commitment. For the sake of our party, for the sake of our country, for the sake of our future, I ask you to march again, the way we marched before."

IV

DOES HE THINK
HE COULD GRAB
THE BRASS RING?

A S MIGHT be expected from the way the speech was interrupted by applause earlier, there was a standing ovation for Kennedy after he took his seat. I was intrigued by the last line that he slipped across to his audience, asking them to "march again, the way we marched before." Did he mean to suggest by that, I mused, the possibility of another Kennedy candidacy? He had dropped a similar hint in the introduction to this speech when he said, "You and I remember 1960, when President Kennedy came to Salt Lake City to seek the Presidency." Hearing that I wondered if Ted Kennedy were following in his brother's footsteps for the same reason. And I wondered, also, if he had made the remark precisely to inspire such wondering.

The next morning, while addressing a crowd of about a

thousand students at the University of Utah College of Law, there were even more striking hints, and these seemed clearly calculated to arouse speculation as to the possibility of Kennedy's candidacy. One such hint came across with special poignancy. After starting off by deploring the fact that the mood of the campuses has become "uncomfortably reminiscent of the Silent Generation of the 50s," Kennedy exhorted the students to meet their responsibilities as concerned citizens. Rising to an emotional pitch, he declared, "You are the inheritors of the legacy of your brothers and sisters . . ." Suddenly his voice warbled out of control. He stopped, fighting to regain composure, then completed the sentence in a tortured growl: ". . . who asked themselves . . . what they could do . . . for their country . . . in the 60s." A minute or two later when he finished his speech the students gave him a standing ovation.

Even if Kennedy had not choked up while delivering that line, it would have been perfectly plain to everyone in the audience that he had himself in mind when he spoke of doing something with "the legacy of your brothers." One of the students, naturally enough, asked in the question period: "If you say *we* have a responsibility, Senator, then don't *you* have a responsibility to run for President?" The students applauded that. Kennedy, by now composed, milked the situation for all it was worth. First, he got a solid laugh by pretending to dodge the question, calling for the next question. Then, turning serious, he said he would not run, adding, "I intend to fulfill my responsibilities by speaking out in the Senate." And finally, although he could easily have avoided it, Kennedy allowed the student to get the last word. "That's the first statement you've made, Senator," the student said with great fervor, "that I cannot agree with." More applause.

It was a litany I was to hear again and again throughout the trip—Kennedy dropping hints that he was thinking of running (the hints became more blatant as time went on) only to quash speculation with a denial in a question period or at the next airport press conference. At times I was annoyed by watching him get people worked up, only to make them look like fools a short while later. (A few reporters were placed in similar situations when they returned to their offices bursting with the news that "Kennedy is running!" only to have their stories pooh-poohed by editors who had been reading Kennedy's official-sounding denials of candidacy.) It would, of course, be unfair to be too harsh with Kennedy for playing this game. After all, he is wrestling with one of the most difficult decisions a man has ever had to make, a decision that could well be a matter of life or death for him, and one that, given the political institutions and folkways of the American people, simply cannot be reached without preliminary testing and experimentation.

Later that evening, Governor Rampton held a private reception for Kennedy and about a dozen of the state's leading Democrats at the Governor's Mansion. The press was barred, but I later learned that Kennedy had talked quite frankly about how tough he thought Nixon was going to be to beat in 1972. The President's only real vulnerability, I was told Kennedy said, is that "he has so many balls in the air—his travels, dimming the war, and the economy—he may not be able to keep them all up. If Nixon drops one, then maybe the Democrats can take him, but it doesn't look likely right now."

That is not quite the same as saying that Nixon is "unbeatable," as a Washington newspaper recently reported Kennedy to have said. But it did make me understand one central reason why Kennedy cherishes, and is unlikely to relinquish if he can help it, his option to pull out of the running if Nixon seems like a sure winner. Why, from Kennedy's point of view, should he risk his life running in an election no Democrat could win? The irony of this, of course, is that if Nixon looks easy to beat in July, a deadlocked convention might well settle for Humphrey or Muskie; whereas, if Nixon looks almost invincible, the power brokers would realize that only what *Newsweek* chortlingly calls "that old Jack magic" could save the day, and would turn to Kennedy. And if they really came after Kennedy in earnest, he might not—despite what he says about his "insights into the realities of, you know, national politics"—be able to exercise his option to say no.

On the other hand, Kennedy's belief that Nixon will be extremely difficult to beat this year may be a product of wishful thinking. That is, the most desirable of all possible scenarios from Kennedy's point of view may very well be the one in which the Democrats nominate Senator Edmund Muskie at their convention in July—and then Nixon defeats Muskie in November. That would dispose of Muskie and, by 1976, Nixon, too, since the President would be constitutionally barred from seeking a third term. The country would probably be ready for a Democratic President after eight years of a Republican Administration, and Kennedy would thus appear to have a clear field for becoming the 38th President of the United States in 1976. He would have more experience by then, and

Chappaquiddick and the assassinations would be that much further behind him.

While this scenario looks good on paper, the course of real events may be very different indeed. Muskie could get the nomination and win. Mayor John V. Lindsay or someone else might rise to prominence in the Democratic party. Or any of a number of other imponderables could eclipse Kennedy's position. Accordingly, no matter how tantalized he might be with the possibilities of 1976 as a launching date for his Presidential effort, Kennedy is obliged to keep a close watch on the national scene and maintain a position of readiness to seize a good opportunity to gain the White House whenever and however it may present itself. One of the politicians I spoke with who had attended the meeting with Kennedy and Governor Rampton, and who is a genuine Kennedy confidant, made this clear in a conversation we had the next morning over breakfast.

"All things considered," he told me, "Kennedy's best option is to do exactly what he's doing—move out a little bit now and then, and keep in touch with his friends around the country. He'll *never* turn down a draft. I *know* that."

"But do you think, considering the risks, that he really wants to try for it this year?" I asked, and then explained that my talk with Kennedy on the plane had left me with the impression that he might rather wait and try for the White House in 1976 or perhaps even 1980.

"That's possible," came the reply, "but he knows there may be new faces by 1976. He also knows there are kids who will be voting for the first time in 1972 who were six years old when his brother was inaugurated, and that in 1976 there will be a lot more voters who don't even remember Bobby. So maybe 1972 is his best chance."

The remark put me in mind of something Eric Sevareid once said about Kennedy on the CBS Evening News. "His great handicap," Sevareid had commented, "is that while he is still young, the Kennedy drama is already old. New heroes arise to gather the people's love and fascination." Yes, I thought to myself, Kennedy may well be aware of how fleeting is public adoration, and he may well be preparing to make his move this year accordingly.

"Let me tell you a story," my Utah informant continued. "In 1968, Bobby asked a colleague in the Senate if he thought he should run for President. The Senator said no, because he did not think there was any chance Bobby could beat Lyndon Johnson. Then Bobby asked if he thought he should run anyway, for the sake of principle. The Senator said no again, because losing would not prove anything. Then Bobby said—referring to the game you play riding a merry-go-round—'Yeah, but maybe . . . *maybe I could grab the brass ring.*' "

"What is that supposed to prove?" I asked.

My informant looked me in the eye. "Ted's made the same way," he said, measuring his words. "Maybe he thinks *he* could grab the brass ring."

D ENVER, COLORADO—The atmospheric pressure drops almost half a pound per square inch between the Great Salt Lake and the Mile High City, and Presidential politics for Kennedy went through a similar decompression. As before, the press was on hand at the airport to ask him if he had come to announce his candidacy, but not a single political bigwig showed up to encourage him to answer in the affirmative. The welcoming committee consisted of whimsically smiling Willy Schaeffler, the Austrian-born head coach of the United States Ski Association, and an old skiing buddy of all the Kennedy brothers; another old Kennedy-family retainer; and finally John W. Douglas, the tall, graying and somewhat austere son of former Senator Paul Douglas who served as an assistant attorney general in the Justice Department when Bobby was running it and who continues to be a close friend of the Kennedy family. The explanation for the dearth of pols was that this is Muskie country, and not one major politician in the state was anxious to be photographed beside Kennedy, especially just one day before the Senator from Maine happened to be due in town.

As was the case in Salt Lake City, Kennedy's reason for being here was plausible enough. His friend John Douglas was serving as president of the National Legal Aid and Defender Association, a group of liberal lawyers dedicated to making legal services accessible to the poor, and Douglas had asked Kennedy, who has long been interested in the aims of this group and is a member of the Senate Judiciary Committee, to address its annual conference. Fine, but Kennedy opened his speech in the banquet hall of the Denver Hilton with a crack. "I've always wanted to stand before a great convention like this," he said, "but even though this is the wrong one in the wrong city in the wrong year, I'm glad to be here." Much laughter and applause. Now that, to be sure, was merely a joke, and jokes, precisely because they can be laughed off, are not generally considered a respectable sort of evidence in a sober discussion of national politics. But I submit that when Kennedy makes a quip like that on a junket around the country which is arousing speculation he insists he does not wish to encourage, one can only conclude either that the man possesses an uncontrollably mischievous turn of mind or that he is telling less than the whole truth about his intentions.

There was another telltale sign, too. Kennedy's address turned out to be a blistering attack on William H. Rehnquist, whom Kennedy, as a member of the Senate Judiciary Committee, had been examining in Washington two days earlier. Rehnquist had gone on record as saying that Congress and the courts need not concern themselves with wire-tapping by federal investigative agencies, and Kennedy attacked him on that point. A text of Kennedy's address was released in Washington by his Senate office, but the speech he delivered in Denver, and which was released to the press here, revealed that some strong language had been deleted at the last minute. One cut, for example, was a line saying that a study of Rehnquist's views teaches "what 1984 will really be, for ourselves and for our children." I asked Kennedy why he dropped the line. He said that on reflection it sounded "too cute." It did, of course. It was also strident. But the interesting point was that here in conservative Muskie country Kennedy was being careful, extra careful I thought, not to sound too radical. Maybe he *does* think, I pondered as we raced back to the airport for the next leg of the journey, that he can grab the brass ring.

V

THE SUPERSTAR
SHOWS HIS STUFF

SIOUX FALLS, SOUTH DAKOTA—This rough and
ready cow town was Denver in reverse. Here there
were more pols than plain people. At the airport they
fawned on Kennedy and later in the evening they cranked
his arm and surreptitiously fingered his wife's expensive
clothes. All but scrambling aboard our Western Airlines
727 to slap Kennedy on the back was Billy Dougherty, the
sandy-haired, boyish-looking 39-year-old lieutenant governor of the state, who radiates innocence and cornball
charisma like a Saturday night TV celebrity and who plans
to put it all to work later this year knocking off the now
enfeebled old warhorse Senator Karl Mundt.

Billy was the fellow back in 1968 who swaggered into the
Senate Office Building in a big white cowboy hat and told

Bobby Kennedy that he planned to enter his name in the South Dakota Presidential primary. "Get rid of him! I don't care what you do with him! Throw him out a window!" Bobby had shouted at his staff, but a few weeks later, after Bobby had made up his mind to run, he sent a trusted staff man out to South Dakota to help Billy with the job. The returns came in the same day as those from the California primary—the day he was shot—and one of the last things Bobby ever heard was that Billy had pulled off a miracle in South Dakota, winning for him a remarkable 49.7 per cent of the vote in a three-way race.

And Kennedys don't forget. So here was Ted Kennedy coming out to speak at another $25-a-plate roast beef dinner to do a good turn for this gutsy little livestock salesman who had done so well by his brother.

It all added up neatly, a little too neatly perhaps. Standing discreetly in the airport waiting room was South Dakota's Governor Richard S. Kneip, a tall, dark man in his early 40s who has a way of lowering his head and peeping up at you that calls to mind a young Lyndon Johnson. "This is George McGovern country," said Governor Kneip, when I asked him in whose pocket the local delegates were to be found. When pressed, however, he acknowledged that he was "after all, a political realist," adding, in pure Lyndonese, "Don't you seeee? George is our *Senator.*"

And what if George loses the Wisconsin primary in April? "Well, we'll have to wait and seeee."

We didn't have to wait that long. Kennedy had been announced as the principal speaker at the "Lieutenant Governor Billy Dougherty Recognition Dinner" in the Sioux Falls Coliseum that evening, and 1,000 people (200 more than there was food for) showed up to hear him. Billy took the floor first, and in a flash of impromptu-sounding—but more likely calculated—exuberance, drew a roar of applause when instead of introducing Kennedy he practically nominated him. "You talk about unity," said Billy, all smiles. "And I'd like to say one thing. I think we have here one man in this country who can bring this country together. And his name is Senator Edward Kennedy!" That produced a full minute of applause, and not a few hiked-up eyebrows, too, because aside from his big white cowboy hat, Billy wears the hat of the state's national committeeman.

Kennedy thanked Billy for the kind words, and did not trouble to disclaim his alleged powers of unification. Instead, he opened with a spate of nostalgia that made many a tough cattleman's eye begin to water: "No member of my family could return to South Dakota and not express to you the warmth we feel for the support you showed my brother Bob in 1968. I remember speaking with him on the day the returns came in, and how gratified he was not only for the returns themselves but to have had a chance to meet the people of this state. And so, tonight I want to extend a warm word of appreciation from me and the members of my family. And for the times you welcomed my brother Bob to your hearts and homes I want to thank you." The applause was tremendous. Then Kennedy gave them the "forgotten promises" speech and that went over big with the wranglers, too.

Afterwards, to allow for more politicking, there was a reception at the Howard Johnson Motor Inn out on Highway 38. "This was a very remarkable evening," I was told by Congressman Frank Denholm, a tall and rather grave man in his late 40s. "These are conservative and puritanical people you saw tonight, and their enthusiasm shows you that they just aren't thinking about Chappaquiddick any more." A couple of other rather canny-seeming politicos told me that Billy had "nominated" Kennedy to get back at McGovern because McGovern had still not made up his mind between Billy and a freshman congressman named James Abourezk, who also had his eye on Mundt's Senate seat. But that wasn't very convincing. Billy Dougherty struck me as being, for all his wiliness, devoted to the cause of the Kennedys.

I buttonholed Billy and asked him if he thought Kennedy was running.

"Well, ya know," he replied, a conspiratorial hush coming over his voice, "I told Ted tonight he can pick up *all the marbles* if he wants 'em."

Did he mean the delegation from this state would support Kennedy?

"That's what I said."

What was Kennedy's reply?

"Well, ya know . . . He doesn't say anything much. He kinda listens."

SOMEWHERE OVER THE DAKOTAS—Kennedy chartered a little white Falcon fan-jet to take him from Sioux Falls, South Dakota to Bismarck, North Dakota. The same airplane was later to pick him up in St. Paul, Minnesota to ferry him back to Washington.

The little jet flung itself into the icy air, gave us a few hard bumps ("Geez, these little planes are bouncy!") , and then straightened out. I mentioned to Kennedy that I understood that aside from Billy Dougherty quite a number of politicians he had talked with on this trip had asked him to run for President.

"Oh, not many," he replied, obviously discomfited. "I ran into a few friends in Colorado and they expressed interest. They wanted to know what my plans are and will be."

I said I understood he had received a number of written pledges of support from top party leaders in Utah.

"Yes, a few," he said.

And how had Kennedy replied to these letters?

"I say to them I'm going to be active in terms of the direction the party is moving, and in my concerns in the field of foreign affairs."

Loye Miller, Jr., of Knight Newspaper Syndicate, who was also hunched in the cabin, asked Kennedy about his having said he would not endorse any candidate until the convention.

"What I meant to say," Kennedy explained, "is that I will not endorse a candidate until the convention has a nominee."

"Does that mean you'll stay out of it completely?" Miller asked.

"Yes."

"But you'll be a delegate yourself, won't you?"

"No, I don't think so."

"What if Muskie is really sailing by June and the party wants to do it by acclamation. Wouldn't you endorse him then?"

"No. In that case, he wouldn't need my help."

BISMARCK, NORTH DAKOTA—An intense low pressure system near Hudson Bay in Canada that funneled very cold air and winds gusting up to 38 miles per hour conspired to drive the chill factor down to 41 degrees below zero when our little Falcon touched down at the airstrip. So naturally there were lots of jokes all day long about the "cold reception," and about Kennedy's coming to test "not the water but the ice." But apart from the weather, North Dakota's reception was anything but chilly. In fact, the locals went wild over him, and indeed this was the point along the way that the trip took on the unmistakable character of a Presidential campaign.

Ostensibly, Kennedy was here to look in on an Indian training center in connection with his chairmanship of the Senate subcommittee on Indian affairs and to dedicate the Kennedy Memorial Center, which turned out to be the state's Democratic Party headquarters (not a bad break for a young Senator trying to make a name for himself). But Kennedy's deeds as well as words suggested that he really had bigger fish to fry. He spent less than an hour with the Indians—listening to a Chippewa chant performed by a couple of old-timers, accepting a peace pipe and tomahawk from an Indian named Dale Little Soldier, who then gave Joan a kiss, prompting Kennedy to make a quip that almost brought down the teepee: "If he does that again I'm gonna have to use this hatchet!" And Kennedy devoted less than half an hour to the Kennedy Memorial Center, which, it developed, was scarcely in need of the ribbon-cutting dedication that was staged for his arrival, since the center has been open and operating for the past two years.

The greater part of his day was devoted to what reporters like to call a whirlwind tour (considering the weather, the phrase was apt) of press conferences, a luncheon at which he gave the "forgotten promises" speech, a cocktail reception with influential Democrats who will control the state's delegation to the nominating convention in July, and private meetings with high-powered types like Governor William L. Guy, an elegant-looking man who later told me, "I certainly don't discount Senator Kennedy as a possible candidate for the Presidency. A tour such as this certainly keeps delegates and committeemen hanging loose." Another individual Kennedy went into a huddle with was Gorman King, the state's short, hefty national committeeman, who told me that he, too, believed that Kennedy had come in quest of delegates. King added that back in August he had heard that Kennedy was definitely not interested in the nomination, but his latest intelligence from the same source was that Kennedy was very much available for a draft. Who was the source of King's information? A local newspaper publisher. And who, I asked the publisher in turn, had been *his* source of information? A Boston chain-store operator, a Kennedy friend. A call to ask this man who *his* source had been—perhaps the Senator himself?—resulted in a no-comment reply.

T HE CLIMAX of Kennedy's visit to North Dakota, and the appearance at which he most clearly "blew his cover," was his address that afternoon to about 1,000 delegates to the National Farmers Organization Convention in a giant cattle barn called the Bismarck Civic Center. It was Presidential politics all the way. Kennedy said how proud he was to be addressing "this great organization" and how grateful he was "for the warmth that was always expressed to me and the members of my family in North Dakota," and assured everyone that "the people of North Dakota have always had a warm place in the hearts of my family." Then he went after Nixon's farm policy with scythelike swings, and since the audience was all too keenly aware that farm prices were at their lowest since the Depression years, they hoorayed him point by point.

This was no off-the-cuff greeting to old friends, but a major campaign address, the sort of speech a man makes when he is going after the "farm vote." It had no connection with Kennedy's special interests in the Senate. It had no relation to his excuse for being in the state. And it was all beautifully planned and polished, bristling with carefully researched facts and resounding with ringing rhetoric. For example:

"President Kennedy once said, 'The farmer is the only man in our economy who buys everything he buys at retail, sells everything he sells at wholesale, and pays the freight both ways.' (Applause) That has not changed. And in the past two and one half years it has gotten worse. In two and one half years, 100,000 farms have disappeared across this nation. In two and one half years, 595,000 farm residents have left the fields. In two and one half years, farm machinery costs have climbed 13 per cent, farm wages have climbed 14 per cent—but farm prices have barely crept up 3 per cent. Neither plague, nor drought, nor natural disaster could have done as much damage to the American farmer as an indifferent national policy has done over two and one half years." (Prolonged applause).

Once he had finished with the Administration's record, Kennedy spelled out his own farm program. (In case anyone wondered why a Massachusetts Senator, who was not a candidate for President, had any farm program at all, Kennedy had contrived a not too convincing answer. "If you do not produce wheat and if you do not obtain adequate income for what you produce, then my state will not be able to sell its fish products or textiles to the people of the Midwest.") The Kennedy program, it turned out, was as well worked out as his attack on the Administration; it consisted of four points leading up to what he called "a national rural economic development policy" which would provide, among other things, a $20 billion development loan fund available for rural America over the next decade.

Kennedy's peroration (not included in the copies of the speech distributed to the press) was a summons to bring back the New Frontier, and he delivered it with an oro-tund Rooseveltian cadence that brought the farmers to their feet. "The discontent," he said, "is as great as it was ten years ago when the Democratic Administration came to Washington. *That* Administration listened to the people and not to the special interests. *That* Administration awakened this country to meet the challenges at home and abroad. It is time to rekindle that spirit. It is time to call together again the daring and the unreconciled. It's time to march again. Thank you." The applause was thunderous and prolonged. I jotted down in my notebook "He's running," and soon I found I was not alone in having that reaction. Mrs. Liv Bjorlie, the state's savvy national com-mitteewoman who had been tight-lipped before was now exclaiming: "He gave a Presidential speech!"

When we arrived at the airport a few minutes later, the waiting room was fairly bulging with several hundred peo-ple, most of them young. Kennedy struggled up on a chair. "Anybody wanna hear a speech?" The response was ear-splitting. He gave them a few fragments of the Utah Law School speech and then pressed his way to the door. Out-side, as I jogged with Kennedy toward our plane, Richard

Ista, the red-haired and freckle-faced chairman of the state's Democratic party, came trotting along too. A few hours earlier, like Mrs. Bjorlie, he had been cautiously neutral about the various candidates, but now he was jubilant. "Does this answer your question?" Ista shouted into my ear over the scream of the jet engines. "I've never seen anything like this around here! Muskie could never draw like this!"

ST. PAUL, MINNESOTA—The stop in "Minnesoter," according to Kennedy, was just an afterthought, but it seemed more like a carefully prepared denouement once events began to unfold. To start with, the political brass was all there with bells on at the airport when we arrived—Minnesota's lean, young Governor Wendell Anderson and his wife; Senator Walter "Fritz" Mondale and his wife; Democratic state chairman Richard Moe, a handful of congressmen and a throng of reporters and well wishers.

A short while later, Minnesota's Junior Senator, Hubert H. Humphrey, was basking in the spotlight of a cocktail reception for about 500 moneyed Democrats at the St. Paul Hilton when suddenly, at the entrance, TV flood lights popped on, photographers began jumping on chairs and shooting off flash bulbs and all eyes shifted from Humphrey because, yes, the Kennedys had arrived!

The two non-candidates worked their way together and Hubert started telling a long story to Joan Kennedy. It seems Hubert had been in Austin, Minnesota, earlier in the day to dedicate a power plant. Kennedy started tugging his wife's arm to get away, but she was listening in mock-rapt attention and wouldn't budge. "Well," continued Hubert, "the chill factor had brought it down to four below, and so I told them this is a historic moment. I want you to know that Mr. Nixon put on the freeze, but this is *too* cold. I'm gonna make a *short* speech!" Kennedy yanked at his wife's arm again, to no avail. "That's just what I told them. I'm gonna make a *short* speech. And I did, by golly, I said exactly one hundred words. Just *one hundred words*. Now what d'ya think of that?"

Joan roared with laughter as Kennedy practically dismembered her, charging over to the other side of the ballroom and bringing with him about 550 people and leaving with Humphrey, by generous estimate, about four.

And so it went. That night, before an audience of 5,000 in the Municipal Auditorium at a fund-raising rally for the Democratic Farmer-Labor Party, Humphrey got 20 seconds of applause and Kennedy got 40. Humphrey told old jokes—"Somebody said we oughta get behind the President; I said I can't tell which way he's facing"—that fell flat. Kennedy's coy games in the introduction to another rendition of the "forgotten promises" speech—"I've often dreamed of addressing a big convention hall; unfortunately, this isn't the right city or the right year"—had them cheering and stamping and vigorously pumping "Teddy in '72" signs up and down in the balconies. After it was over, Humphrey strolled out in near solitude while Kennedy was clawed by throngs of admirers for 20 minutes. The huge size of the crowd, the feeling of excitement—these were indeed of Presidential character.

Since St. Paul was Kennedy's last appearance on the trip, I began to collect my thoughts about what the future might hold for him. My guess was then, and remains, that Kennedy will now pull back from his relatively active candidacy for fear of having been too open about it already. He will not make any more trips of this kind for a while, and he may encourage a few friends, like Senator John Tunney of California and Governor John Gilligan of Ohio, to throw their support behind other candidates for the time being. I do not expect him to enter any of the primaries, either. Kennedy will watch and wait, although, of course, he will keep making strong statements on the issues that interest him—"putting the blowtorch to the other candidates," as he expresses it, using his forward position to force them to take strong positions, too. If Muskie or someone else gathers strength in the primaries, or if Nixon begins to look even tougher to beat than Kennedy now thinks he is, Kennedy will assuredly try to pull out of the running with an unequivocal statement of non-candidacy. On the other hand, if the primaries generate hostilities and commit a substantial but not nearly sufficient number of delegates to one or another candidate, then I expect Kennedy to step up the pace of his activity and, when he walks into the convention at Miami Beach in July, the balloons may very well go up—and, soon after, he will be heard asking the country to help him finish what his brothers began.

A FTER THE ST. PAUL rally, Kennedy and his wife were due to be picked up by the Falcon they had chartered to fly them home to Washington. I had arranged to take a commercial flight back to New York the next morning, but I went out to the Twin Cities International Airport with Mondale, Anderson and their wives to say goodbye to Kennedy. Kennedy invited us all into the Falcon for a farewell drink. The cabin was so small we had to put our heads together as if in a football huddle, but spirits were high and the booze flowed. Kennedy began to unwind a bit and I could see for the first time what a strain he must have been under, telling at least 40 people a day that he was not running for President.

Soon we piled out and watched through car windows as the white Falcon sped down the runway, leaped with astonishing suddenness into the night sky and slowly turned east. The path of the plane took it just under a thin sliver of moon that seemed to be hanging out there in the night, and I thought for a moment that if I were asked to describe the passing of those two objects in the sky I would say that Kennedy's plane looked like a finger reaching out for a partially obscured brass ring.

Part
TWO

AFTER
CHAPPAQUIDDICK

VI

THE
INCREDIBLE CONFESSION

E DWARD KENNEDY'S television address to the people of Massachusetts on July 25, 1969, in which he told of his conduct after the automobile accident on the island of Chappaquiddick, was one of the most devastating confessions an American public figure ever made. And then it was not believed.

There are, of course, a number of reasons why. To begin with, the circumstances surrounding the accident included all the elements needed to stimulate gossip—a handsome young man and an attractive young woman alone together on a back road late at night, a drowning, mysterious and inconsistent behavior, the suggestion of a conspiracy to evade the law, and the spectacle of a glamorous career brought down in shame and disgrace. Once the gossip began to flow, nothing could stop it. Almost everyone who followed the news in those days soon developed a personal theory about what *really* happened at Chappaquiddick, and others came forward with tall stories about Kennedy's supposed moral transgressions in the past which, if true, would tend to substantiate the most lurid notions about what took place on that little island with the long, curious Indian name.

In the second place, the story Kennedy related seemed so bizarre as to defy common sense. What, for example, were a group of six men, most of them married, doing at a summer cookout with six young women, all of them unmarried? Why had Kennedy and Mary Jo Kopechne left the party early? And why, after the fatal accident, did Kennedy swim alone with all his clothes on (even his shoes!) across a dangerous channel? There seemed in all this something decidedly fishy.

Next, the reason Kennedy's confession was not accepted as the whole truth was that his mishandling of the politics of the situation was a blunder almost as great as the accident itself. He seemed to stall too long before being willing to face the public and answer questions. Also, one could not help but become suspicious on reading in the newspapers that the old Kennedy brain trust—men such as Theodore Sorensen, Richard Goodwin and even former Secretary of Defense Robert McNamara—had converged on the family compound at Hyannis Port to help Kennedy plan (or plot, it seemed) what to say.

In addition to that, the speech itself sounded false, employing as it did a species of demagoguery reminiscent of Richard Nixon's "Checkers" speech of 1952. Kennedy's assertion that he was tortured by "whether some awful curse did actually hang over all the Kennedys" was making use of sensationalism to mask irrelevancy just as was the case when Nixon dragged his wife and his black and white spaniel into the Checkers speech, with references to his wife's "respectable Republican cloth coat" and the fact that "Pat is not a quitter. After all, her name was Patricia Ryan and she was born on Saint Patrick's Day, and you know the Irish never quit." And Kennedy's peroration, in which he suddenly and illogically began to sound as if he were about to make some noble and heroic sacrifice seemed as dubious as the moral posturing of Nixon's speech. Also, both speeches concluded with an appeal for expressions of support—a demagogic trick since in both cases the aim clearly was to stimulate a torrent of letters and telegrams which would give a semblance of public support without, of course, being the least bit representative of public opinion as a whole. Yet the similarities between the two "confessions" go no further. Nixon, after all, sought to *justify* his use of a special fund that had been created for him by a group of wealthy backers, whereas Kennedy acknowledged that his behavior had been "indefensible."

Here, with the rhetoric and posturing stripped away (Theodore Sorensen, by the way, was the chief ghost writer of the speech) is what Kennedy said. He began by telling his audience that he had just entered a plea of guilty to the charge of leaving the scene of an accident in which Miss Mary Jo Kopechne, a passenger in his car, was killed. He had been driving with her at night on an unlit road on the island of Chappaquiddick, he said, when his car plunged off a narrow bridge, overturned and immediately filled with water. The water entered his lungs and, "I actually felt the sensation of drowning," he said. He alone struggled to the surface. He made "repeated efforts" to rescue Mary Jo by diving into the "strong and murky current," but succeeded only in "increasing my state of utter exhaustion and alarm." He then walked back to the cottage where a party was still in progress that he and Mary Jo had left, and where, instead of telephoning the authorities for help, he asked his cousin Joseph Gargan and a friend, Paul Markham, to return with him to the scene of the accident to make a new effort to locate the girl, who was then presumably dead. The three men returned to the bridge, dove into the water but were unable to recover the body. At about that point, Kennedy lost control of himself.

"I was overcome, I'm frank to say," he declared on television, "by a jumble of emotions, grief, fear, doubt, exhaustion, panic, confusion and shock."

He then commanded his friends to drive him to the ferry slip, threw himself into the water again, swam to the main island of Martha's Vineyard—nearly drowning in the process—made it to his hotel room and collapsed. He got up once in the middle of the night, but went back to bed and did not report the accident until the next morning.

Kennedy's doctor later told him that he had suffered a mild cerebral concussion in the accident—an injury that commonly results in the temporary impairment of judgment—but, Kennedy told his television audience, "I do not seek to escape responsibility for my actions by placing the blame either in the physical or emotional trauma brought on by the accident." His conduct was, he declared, "indefensible."

I call this confession devastating (once it has been sorted out from the rest of the speech) because in it Kennedy acknowledged almost all the wrongdoing and irresponsibility that his critics have accused him of. If one charges Kennedy

*Senator Kennedy speaking at the Kennedy
Memorial Center in Bismarck, North Dakota,
on a political trip in November 1971.*

The Kennedy family at Hyannis Port in 1934.
Rear: Eunice, John, Kathleen and Rosemary.
Front: Joseph Jr., Mrs. Kennedy, Robert, Edward,
Mr. Kennedy, Patricia and Jean.

Above: John Kennedy proposing a toast at a reception following his brother Edward's marriage to the former Joan Bennett. Below: The Kennedy brothers at Hyannis Port after the Democratic convention of 1960.

*President Kennedy's widow, flanked by the
President's brothers, arriving for the
funeral at St. Matthew's Cathedral
in Washington in November 1963.*

*Above: Senators Robert and Edward Kennedy
attending a subcommittee hearing in 1965.
Below: Following a nearly-fatal plane crash in 1964,
Kennedy and his wife Joan at a Boston hospital.*

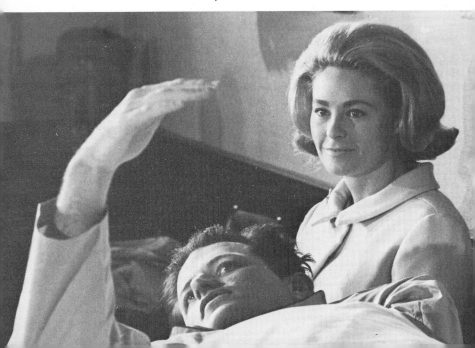

The Kennedy brothers outside the Capitol
after Edward's return to the Senate
in January 1965.

Kennedy eulogizing his brother Robert at St. Patrick's Cathedral in June 1968. Robert's coffin is draped with the flag.

*Kennedy at work
in his Senate office
in February 1969.
Right: The U.S.S.
Joseph P. Kennedy, Jr.*

Kennedy with his best friend,
Senator John V. Tunney, and their wives.

Explaining the
accident at
Chappaquiddick.

*Kennedy talking with the author
in the Boston Public Gardens
in May 1970.*

Campaigning for re-election to
the Senate in 1970. Above, at a
shipboard party. Below, outside
his Charles River home in Boston.

Kennedy on his November 1971 political
tour. Above, in Sioux Falls, South
Dakota. Below, with Wayne Owens (to his
right) in Salt Lake City, Utah.

*Speaking at a political rally
in St. Paul, Minnesota
in November 1971.*

Senator Edward Kennedy seems to ponder the future.

with having panicked in a crisis at Chappaquiddick, Kennedy does not evade the charge. He even used the word "panic" when listing the "jumble of emotions" with which he was "overcome." If one charges that Chappaquiddick reveals him as irresponsible, he admits that "instead of looking directly for a telephone after lying exhausted in the grass for an undetermined time, I walked back to the cottage," and even then did not seek to telephone for help. If one suspects (as I do) that the reason he swam across the channel, returned to his hotel room and then did not report the accident was in order to create an alibi that he had not been in the car at the time of the accident (a strategy rejected the next morning), he provides a veiled acknowledgment of even that in the following words (italics mine):

"All kinds of scrambled thoughts—all of them confused, some of them irrational, many of which I cannot recall and *some of which I would not have seriously entertained under normal circumstances*—went through my mind during this period. They were reflected in the various inexplicable, inconsistent and *inconclusive things I said and did,* including such questions as whether the girl might still be alive somewhere out of that immediate area, whether some awful curse did actually hang over all the Kennedys, *whether there was some justifiable reason for me to doubt what had happened and to delay my report, whether somehow the awful weight of this incredible incident might in some way pass from my shoulders.*"

And finally, if the charge is that Kennedy's conduct demonstrates that he should not be entrusted with the high office of Presidency, he goes his accusers one better, acknowledging: "These events . . . raise the question in my mind of whether my standing among the people of my state has been so impaired that I should resign my seat in the United States Senate."

The one gossipy accusation to which Kennedy would not plead guilty was that he and Mary Jo Kopechne left the party for an "immoral" purpose. "There is no truth, no truth whatever," he told his television audience, "to the widely circulated suspicions of immoral conduct that have been leveled at my behavior and hers regarding that evening." Kennedy did not say in his television speech why he and Mary Jo had left the party, but at the inquest later on he explained that, after talking with Mary Jo "for perhaps some minutes," he noticed it was 11:15 P.M. and told her that he had had enough of the party and was going to return by car and ferry to his hotel on the nearby main island of Martha's Vineyard. "She indicated to me she was desirous of leaving, if I would be kind enough to drop her back at her hotel," Kennedy testified at the inquest. "I said," he continued, "Well, I'm leaving immediately," and so they left the party, according to Kennedy's story, to return to their separate lodgings in Edgartown.

But this was not accepted by Massachusetts District Judge James A. Boyle, the 63-year-old Vineyard Republican who presided over the official inquest to ascertain whether or not criminal behavior had taken place. "I infer," Judge Boyle wrote in a twelve-page conclusion to the inquest, ". . . that Kennedy and Kopechne did not intend to return to Edgartown at that time." He cited a number of facts testified to which, he said, led him to doubt Kennedy's story that he was taking Mary Jo to the main island when they left the party. The most important of these seeming inconsistencies were the following: Kennedy's car was not headed toward the ferry slip when it plunged off Dike Bridge; Kennedy drove away with Mary Jo alone, leaving his chauffeur Jack Crimmins at the party; Kennedy told only Crimmins that he was leaving for the night and Mary Jo told no one; Mary Jo did not ask her roommate for the weekend, Esther Newberg, for the key to their room at the Katama Shores Motor Inn in Edgartown; Mary Jo left her pocketbook at the Chappaquiddick cottage; and Kennedy took the larger of the two cars at the cottage, although he knew there were others there who would require transportation later in the evening.

Judge Boyle's conclusion, of course, was merely one man's opinion. The examination of Kennedy and the other witnesses had been cursory, to say the least, and the Judge did not direct his accusation of perjury to be submitted to the test of trial by jury. Furthermore, Judge Boyle had chosen not to limit himself to the standards of "proof beyond a reasonable doubt" that are obtained at all criminal trials; instead, he used the principle of "probable guilt" and "presumption of fact," which he defined as "nothing more than a probable or natural explanation of facts . . . which reasonable men would draw from experience." Kennedy, naturally, disagreed with the Judge's conclusion, replying to the press that he had answered all questions "truthfully" and that the "findings of the Judge's report are not justified and I reject them." Kennedy added that he would have no more to say about the accident at Chappaquiddick since "the facts of this incident are now fully public, and eventual judgment and understanding rests where it belongs . . ."

Further examination of Kennedy and the other witnesses might have explained one or all of the inconsistencies that led Judge Boyle to distrusting Kennedy's story, and it is unfortunate that such questioning was not pressed.* For example, Kennedy's knowledge of the roads of Chappaquiddick and his general driving ability and sense of direction should have been explored in detail. It seems unlikely that on his way to the ferry slip he could have made a wrong turn from a relatively wide, paved road onto a narrow, unpaved one without being aware of it, and yet there are numerous Kennedy family stories about his poor driving ability and befuddled sense of direction. Rita Dallas, who used to be the nurse of the late Joseph Kennedy, Sr., recently recalled how Kennedy once took his father for a drive and got lost. "His sense of direction was always so bad," she recalls, "there was a family joke about his never knowing what turn to take." In addition, it is known that Kennedy habitually drives too fast. When I first heard of the accident at Chappaquiddick, I recall looking up some notes I had made during a conversation about Kennedy's security problem just a few months before. "I'm not nearly so worried about another assassination," a close friend of Kennedy's had told me, "as I am about his crazy driving." Conceivably, such information as this if developed in detail by courtroom examination and cross-examination would have made Kennedy's story believable.

In any case, whether or not Kennedy lied about where he was going when he left the party is really the least important aspect of the incident at Chappaquiddick. His

---

* The case is now considered legally closed, since a Massachusetts Supreme Judicial Court has ruled that the transcripts of such inquests must be kept secret until all possibilities of prosecution have been eliminated. The release to the press of the transcript in this case, therefore, is believed to have foreclosed the possibility of reopening the case.

conduct after the accident is what is most damning, and his admissions concerning it have given him a great deal to live down. What is interesting about that, however, is that, grievous as Kennedy's failings may have been, it is by no means impossible for him to be publicly rehabilitated. As Montaigne said, worthy men can survive their reputations—both overblown and scandalous. Indeed the annals of American politics offer numerous illustrations of men who have regained public confidence after making some colossal blunders. Robert Kennedy, to cite one example, lived down his reputation as a McCarthyite (he actually *worked* for the late Senator Joseph McCarthy's subcommittee) and later became the darling of the chic radicals for whom McCarthyism was next to satanism. Harold Hughes, the junior Senator from Iowa and a former state governor, has lived down his reputation as a drunkard. Richard Nixon has survived his reputation as a smear artist, a hatchet man, a Congressman in the pay of Big Business— indeed what *hasn't* he lived down? Grover Cleveland even went on to be elected the 22nd President of the United States after it was revealed that he had fathered an illegitimate son.* In short, it would appear that public men may

---

* Soon after the Democrats nominated Cleveland for President in 1884, a Buffalo newspaper revealed that, years before, Cleveland had had an affair with a widow—a certain Mrs. Halpin. Cleveland had encouraged the woman to believe he would marry her, had fathered an illegitimate son and had then committed the child to an orphan asylum. At first, Cleveland prepared a detailed confession; then, however, acting on the advice of his campaign manager, he assumed a dignified silence. Later, through spokesmen, he let it be known that while he doubted that he was the father of Mrs. Halpin's son, he might have been, and thus he had accepted responsibility for the child and provided for the boy's support and education. The resulting scandal was thus minimized and did not stop Cleveland from being elected President.

live down almost any transgression so long as they are given time, possess sufficient strength of character and have within them a knack for doing penance in public.

Oddly enough, the profession of journalism which joins so avidly in the destruction of reputations, also, perhaps necessarily, cooperates when the occasion calls for their rehabilitation. Thus, after a period of exposure and vilification, journalists discover the "older, wiser, more mellow" Robert Kennedy, the "bigger, more self-assured" Lyndon Johnson, the "new" Nixon. It is as if journalism, which made hero worship untenable, created in its place a new mythology—the moral equivalent of the Horatio Alger story in which naughty boys, once shamed, grow into good and noble men.

VII

HOW GRAVE
IS THE WOUND?

WASHINGTON, D.C.—If, then, the public is at least potentially capable of forgiving Kennedy for Chappaquiddick, the question remains: Can Kennedy forgive himself? Did the experience compromise his self-esteem or commitment to public life? Not just politically, but personally, how grave was the wound? In order to find out answers to these questions, I began a series of talks with Kennedy in the spring of 1970 just prior to and immediately after publication of the transcript of the inquest into the accident at Chappaquiddick.

At first, all I was able to pick up from those around him were intriguing and often sobering hints and suggestions as to the extent of his injury. For example, a Massachusetts Congressman who had recently had a number of dealings with him told me that Kennedy seemed unusually pre-occupied. "Whenever I am with him," this Congressman said, "I get the feeling that he is constantly thinking of other things—that his mind is somewhere else."

A close friend of Kennedy's who attended the party at Chappaquiddick confirmed this view. "I can always tell his mood. The twinkle is there today," he remarked one day in Boston as we were watching Kennedy address a local advertising club in a warm-up for his 1970 campaign for re-election to the Senate. "But at other times," this friend continued, "I can see by the way he tightens his jaw and grits his teeth that he's thinking of those things he's been through."

In Washington, Senator Mike Mansfield, the Democratic majority leader with whom Kennedy had been working closely in his capacity as majority whip, also spoke of his young colleague's distractedness. "There are moments," Mansfield told me, "when shadows fall across his face. It happens now and again. Not when he talks about his brothers. He has steeled himself in those areas. But at certain times, for no palpable reason, he will withdraw into himself. Not for long—just for a few moments. Then someone will make a remark and he'll snap out of it. But you know that his mind was on those tragedies."

A Congressman who had always been closer to Bobby Kennedy than to Ted, but who nevertheless saw a good deal of both brothers, told me he thought Kennedy had retreated into a shell since the previous summer. "People not in his intimate circle," he said, "don't see him as much as before. There seems to sit within him the suspicion that one may think differently of him now. Perhaps that's partly why he keeps so much to himself and limits his company predominantly to those he feels secure with."

Kennedy's top Senate aides—the young men, all of them his contemporaries, who were with him more often than anyone else those days—led me yet a step closer to discovering Kennedy's state of mind. One of these aides, the staff man who had doubled as Kennedy's chauffeur around the capital ever since the Senator's driver's license had been suspended after he pleaded guilty to leaving the scene of an accident, declared that he had often heard Kennedy wonder aloud if the woes of his life would ever end "or if they will just go on and on and on."

Another staff member—a key man in the Washington office—talked to me about Kennedy over a drink in a bar across the street from their quarters in the Old Senate Office Building, and kept repeating the phrase "pain and suffering" and such remarks as, "Can you *imagine* what's been going on inside him? Can you *imagine?*" After a second Scotch, he picked the tubular, plastic swizzle stick out of his drink, carefully tied it into a knot, and said, as he drew the knot taut, "Someday his autopsy is going to show some scars that no one—not even *us*—realized were there."

B OSTON, MASSACHUSETTS—I had not spoken with Kennedy for more than a year, not since a few months before Chappaquiddick, and so I had plenty of catching up to do. Nevertheless, all the reading that I did beforehand, all that I learned by talking to those who had been close to him at that time, and indeed all that I gathered from my first few visits with the Senator himself, did little to prepare me for the candid and surprising conversation we had early one morning just three days after publication of the Chappaquiddick transcript. Our conversation took place as we strolled across the Public Gardens in downtown Boston. Kennedy had just delivered an after-breakfast speech on the drug problem to a slightly bleary-eyed gathering of the Massachusetts Teachers Association in the ballroom of one of Boston's new, convention-seeking hotels. Jack Crimmins then drove us in his dark blue Chevy back toward Kennedy's townhouse at the foot of Beacon Hill. Since the weather was fair—showers had been forecast but it was turning out to be a glorious day, in fact, one of the first of the season on which Bostonians could venture forth without jackets—Kennedy asked Crimmins to drop us off at the corner of Commonwealth Avenue and Arlington Street so the two of us could walk together about a mile across the Gardens and down the brick-paved sidewalks of Charles Street to the Senator's home.

"It's really beautiful here, isn't it?" Kennedy remarked, taking a deep sniff of the balmy air as we entered the Gardens. It was. The grass to either side of the meandering path we strolled along was as green as Ireland. Handsome English elms and silver maples showed new leaves the size of a baby's hand. As we approached the swanboat pond, we came upon luxuriantly blooming willow trees; patches of crimson and white tulips and yellow daffodils gave dashes of color to the green grounds.

It was still early in the morning and the Gardens were practically deserted. A couple of young women, wearing slacks and pushing strollers, came up to us; one of them, batting her eyes coquettishly, said, "Hi, Ted." Behind them came a policeman, smiling and swinging his nightstick, who called out in a bold County Clare brogue, "Good marnin', Sinitar." Apart from these passersby, we were alone.

I asked Kennedy if he felt in good spirits. "Well," he said, with a light sigh, "the events of recent years, obviously, weigh heavily. I don't just mean last summer, but everything I've been through in recent years." Had his returning to Massachusetts and plunging into another campaign helped to pick him up a bit? He admitted that it had, but added, "It's a lot more difficult to work up the same enthusiasm as before, given recent events"—again resorting to that impersonal and unspecific phrase with which he has learned to speak of otherwise unmentionable calamities. "I don't mean that campaigning is without rewards," he continued. "I meet people. There is great warmth, and that's always a pleasure to experience. But a lot of the thrill, and the, well, the sort of . . . excitement is gone for me. I expect it to be gone forever."

This comment turned my mind back to the day a week earlier in which we had spent a couple of hours together driving from New Haven to Boston. Kennedy had come to the Yale campus on Earth Day in response to a long-standing invitation to address the undergraduate Political Union. However, the murder-and-kidnapping trial of Bobby Seale and 13 other Black Panthers in New Haven had suddenly threatened to turn Earth Day at Yale into what the militant underground press was billing as "a festival of violence." Most of the student body was already out on strike. The streets were crowded with angry-looking pickets, many of them non-students. A group of Black Panthers, for example, was handing out a leaflet picturing the New Haven chief of police over the headline, "Wanted: Dead—Shoot on Sight."

Congressman Emilio Daddario of Hartford, who was also scheduled to address a group of Yale students later in the day, cancelled his appearance, and one of his aides called

Kennedy's office to suggest that Kennedy, too, would be better off if he passed New Haven by. Despite this warning, and despite his security man's visible agitation, Kennedy stuck to his plan.

As Kennedy stood up behind the microphone in the Freshman Commons to address a capacity audience of about 700 students (at least 500 more were gathered outside), six young men commandeered the dais, forced the Senator to return to his seat and then read statements charging him with "neglect and irresponsibility" and pronouncing him a "Yankee criminal."

When finally permitted to speak, Kennedy said that he was not sufficiently informed about the coming Black Panther trial to comment on the possibility of justice being done. "All I *can* comment on," he said, "is that I do not believe that violence should be employed." As he continued his voice began to tremble: "I am an authority on violence." He paused a moment to regain his composure; the audience was perfectly still. "All it brings is pain and suffering." Another pause. "And there is no place for that in our society."

Kennedy went on, now with fire in his voice: "I think that protest is becoming far too comfortable, like everything else in America . . . We can protest anything now, using the same old procedures, writing on the same old cardboards with detachable handles. If you want to bring an end to war—then work to elect men who agree with you and mount that political campaign this fall that we know was successful before. If you are still insistent on racial equality, then go where you are needed—to register blacks, to assist with their arguments in court, to offer your services to their cause. If you care about poverty, go live it.

Teach the children, work with the addict, help them in their community programs. . . . In short, act in a way meaningful to someone other than yourself."

Kennedy was accorded a standing ovation that continued while he made his way down through the crowded Commons hall and out through the kitchen. Once outside, he was as buoyant as I have ever seen him. Perhaps for the first time since Chappaquiddick, Kennedy had been more in danger from forces without than from forces within; and he had risen to the occasion with gallantry rather than having recoiled in torment.

Just before he stepped into his waiting car, a demonstrator called out to him, "Hey, Kennedy, why don't you sell your car and give the money to the poor?"

"Because I gotta get where I'm going," he barked over his shoulder and popped into the car with his sister, Mrs. Stephen Smith; his cousin, Joseph Gargan; and an old friend, Ray La Rosa. As soon as the car began to move, typical Kennedy-circle badgering broke out. "Hey, Joey," Kennedy sang out merrily to Gargan, who owned the car, a 1967 Plymouth stationwagon, "I didn't know you had such a fancy car. You heard the kid. You gotta sell it now. Gee, I don't know what you can get for this, Joey. You better look around." A few minutes later, Kennedy was reciting one of his subterraneously famous imitations of the way a certain Southern patriarch addresses him: "Kinndy? Kinndy, wha'chew want *now?*"

Walking together in the Public Gardens, I reminded him of his speech at Yale, and of the playfulness in the car afterwards. Hadn't the experience bucked him up, I asked. "Something like New Haven helps," he acknowledged. "There was a supercharged atmosphere there. Yes, their

9 7

response—that gave me a feeling of satisfaction." Then he began speaking with animation. "What I gathered from that was something I'd known before but it was reinforced there. It was that these young people want to be challenged. I tried to do that at the end of my speech. They want to be part of the system. They want this exchange. I somehow got the feeling of great confidence in them."

But what about those who seized the dais? "Well," he said, "any public figure today has to expect this alienation, has to expect these disruptions. I foresee even further polarization—black and white, North and South. You've got high Administration officials playing with these frustrations, playing with the sense of powerlessness. That's the greatest danger. It's a very dangerous trend and it's picking up speed. We have to resist that. What we have to do is get the moderate people to see that this is a time for them to become involved, rather than to allow themselves to be turned off. They're the ones who have the power to change things for the better. We have to get them involved."

I turned the conversation to Chappaquiddick. Judge Boyle had raised a number of questions about the veracity of his testimony at the inquest, I said. Would he care to comment on any of these questions? "I'm not going to do that," Kennedy answered firmly. "Look, every time I say something—for example, that I swam across the channel— fifteen people turn up who say they were in a boat at about that time and they didn't see me swimming. So then I have to explain that. How *can* I explain that? Everything just adds. It just adds. There doesn't seem to be any way to end it."

I mentioned that he had once told Matthew V. Storin of *The Boston Globe* that one day he would reveal the full story of Chappaquiddick, but he had considered it unwise to do so then because the truth would not be believed in what Kennedy regarded as an atmosphere of suspicion. "I did have such a conversation," he acknowledged, "but that was last summer, before the inquest. It's all in the transcript now. So I don't have anything more to say."

I wanted to pursue the matter of his conduct. I said I realized that he himself had termed his actions "indefensible." Nevertheless, the transcript showed that the two doctors who examined him after the accident found "concussion, contusions, and abrasions, acute cervical strain," and Judge Boyle had noted the medical conclusion that "impairment of judgment and confused behavior are consistent with this type of injury." So who was to be believed? Either there was no defense for his conduct, and thus, as some have argued, it is fair to say that Chappaquiddick demonstrated that Kennedy cannot handle himself in a crisis or there *is* a defense for his conduct, and, as others have maintained, it is unfair to judge what Kennedy might do as a high officeholder in some future national emergency on the basis of how he behaved after having his head banged against a windshield and then being nearly drowned in the dark.

"Other people are going to have to resolve that," Kennedy replied. "The issue of this campaign is whether I'm an effective Senator. The people of Massachusetts are going to have to make a judgment whether, in the light of the history of the group of very distinguished Senators who have represented this state in the past, they feel I'm equipped to serve them in the United States Senate." Then he added a little irritably, "Let *them* decide. *They* decide."

We were walking just then past the "ether monument"

—a 40- or 50-foot-tall cluster of pink marble columns, sculpted lions' heads and romantic statuary erected in 1846 to commemorate the discovery, made at Massachusetts General Hospital, that "the inhaling of ether causes insensibility to pain"—and it was then, just by accident, that I happened to ask what proved to be the most painful question of all. I said I had heard a rumor that he was contemplating retirement from public life at some point after the November election—was there any truth to this?

Kennedy had been sober-faced before; now his brow seemed to descend. He has an unusually high and broad forehead. When he is worried, concentrating hard—or pained—his brow falls and his eyes narrow, giving his forehead an even larger, huskier aspect, as if a kind of carapace under which his more sensitive features retreat. He looked this way for a moment, reminiscent of his appearance at the funerals and gravesides of his brothers, but when he spoke his voice was calm. "I've thought about retirement, sure," he said. "And I've made up my mind that if my effectiveness is not there, if my effectiveness has been compromised, I won't stay in public life."

This caught me by surprise. After discussing the retirement rumor with a group of reporters only the night before, I had dismissed it as completely unfounded in fact. I was aware, of course, that in his television speech immediately after the accident at Chappaquiddick, Kennedy had raised the question of whether or not his standing was so impaired that he would resign his Senate seat, but five days later, after having predictably received many thousands of letters, telegrams and phone calls urging him to carry on, his office had issued a terse statement declaring that he had decided to "resume his duties," that he would run for re-election in 1970, and that if returned to the Senate he would "serve out his entire six-year term." With that, it had seemed to me, the question of his retirement had been dispensed with, and so I wondered if he were serious now or if his remark were merely rhetorical. Consequently, I asked if he were satisfied now that he had *not* lost his effectiveness.

"No," he said flatly, starting to walk again. "It's an open question, still an open question. I have a lot of things to go through. There is the election in November. And I have my work in the Senate. We'll have to see how it goes. With the election coming, well, obviously"—he chuckled—"I could retire after that even if I didn't choose to." He became serious once more. "But I don't mean the election is the only thing for me to consider. It's a question of how useful I feel I can be by remaining in public life." You don't mean, I said, that you might make a snap decision about this? "No," he replied. "It's the sort of thing you get a feel for over a period of a year or so."

Just then I recalled that one of Kennedy's aides had remarked to me—although I had not taken it seriously at the time—that the two of them occasionally discussed in a lighthearted, pipe-dreaming sort of way how great it might be to simply drop out. "I'll tell the Senator I saw an ad in the paper that a marina or a chain of hotels is up for sale in the Bahamas or Nantucket," this aide had said, "and that we could go into business together and make a bundle. And he'll say, '*What?* Are you kidding? Hey, that would be *fantastic!*' But, of course, those are just words. That's not for real."

Yet now, hearing Kennedy speak so soberly about the possibility of leaving public life, I began to wonder if there were not some significance to those pipe dreams after all. And so I asked if he had considered any specific retirement plans. "It isn't a question of deciding what else I might do," he answered. "It's a question of whether you stay in public life. That's the fundamental thing. After you make that decision, then—all right—then you decide what you want to do next."

But there it was. Kennedy was seriously thinking of calling it quits. Cynics will be quick to assert that he said this to me as a reporter in order to stimulate support in the then-forthcoming election for the Senate; the threat to retire being a pretty reliable ploy for a politician in trouble —as Kennedy well knew from the reaction to his television speech after Chappaquiddick. The fact was, however, that Kennedy had not been saying anything of this kind in his statements to other reporters in Massachusetts. Furthermore, a few days after I published these remarks of his in *The New York Times Magazine,* Kennedy was interviewed on NBC–TV's *Today Show* and asked about the report that he was "seriously thinking of quitting politics." He replied, "If we're really going to do the things my brothers were interested in, they remain to be done . . . So we're going to continue to be in there, and it's going to take a good Republican this November to lick us." That did not explicitly contradict what he had said to me (namely, that he would decide about remaining in public life *after* the election), but the implication—and Kennedy knew that he could get away with a fuzzy implication in the bland atmosphere of a TV talk show—was to put down speculation that he was thinking of quitting. I feel sure, therefore, that Kennedy did not open up to me that day in the Public Gardens in the hope of gaining something politically, because he did his best to squirm out of affirming what he had said when next asked about it. I think he just very plainly spoke his mind, affording me a rare glimpse of how shaken and hurt he was by Chappaquiddick nearly a year after the accident had taken place. I don't think he was putting me on, either. On this question, only the truth could have inflicted as much pain as he gave evidence of feeling as we strolled past that monument to man's triumph over pain.

It would be quite wrong to conclude from the foregoing that Ted Kennedy was seized with inconsolable grief and gloom upon the publication of Judge Boyle's conclusion to the inquest, or that he went moping about wondering what it would be like to become America's Duke of Windsor. He *was* deeply disturbed; he *was* occasionally distracted, but after having lived with the tragedy for nine months as he had by this time he was beginning to recover his balance and his sense of humor. For example, when Kennedy read the transcript of the inquest, according to one of his aides, he could not withhold a wry chuckle when he came to Gargan's painstakingly detailed explanation of how on the night of the party he went about toasting cheese hors d'oeuvres in the oven without burning them (Gargan prescribes 12 minutes at 450 degrees). Kennedy laughed aloud when he came to his chauffeur's colloquy with the Court about his drinking habits:

THE COURT: Are you a heavy drinker?
THE WITNESS: I am not, Sir.
THE COURT: Are you a light drinker?
THE WITNESS: Three, three drinks.
THE COURT: A day?
THE WITNESS: At *night!* Never drink during the day.

I heard more evidence of Kennedy's somewhat rough-hewn wit in the course of the same weekend during which we had that sober conversation in the Boston Public Gardens. On one occasion when we were riding in a taxicab, a motorcycle policeman almost crashed into the car on Kennedy's side. Kennedy not only flinched, he practically doubled up into a ball. He uncoiled with a laugh, saying, "Jeez, an accident's all I need *now!*" Then he added, "And nobody'd ever believe me when I said how it happened!"

The next evening—the fourth day after the Chappaquiddick transcript had been released—Kennedy was addressing a group of firemen. "I always wanted to be a firefighter, but somehow wound up in public life," he told them. "But after the events of last week I wish I'd *been* a firefighter!" The group roared with laughter. "As a matter of fact," Kennedy went on, "today I *feel* like one." The laughter broke into applause. Kennedy seemed to be having a marvelous time. Then the microphone into which he was speaking went dead. A few seconds later it came sputtering back to life with a series of weird-sounding squeaks and warbles. Kennedy laughed gaily and brought down the house, twitting his Republican opponent, Josiah A. Spaulding. "Hey," he said, "is that Si Spaulding out there strangling a chicken?"

VIII

POLITICAL DECOMPRESSION

WASHINGTON, D.C.—A good part of the reason why Kennedy was able to take with equanimity Judge Boyle's questioning of the veracity of his testimony at the inquest was that Kennedy had long since adjusted to the much heavier blow that befell him when everyone else questioned his story, and when he, accordingly, withdrew from the Presidential stakes. Thereupon, he suffered a sort of instant political decompression. His great power and prestige in the Senate, once supported by the eagerness of his colleagues to join forces with a young man who seemed so likely to occupy the White House sooner or later, and by their desire to curry favor with one who could so readily lend glamor and attract money to their personal causes, collapsed overnight.

Kennedy's record of non-accomplishment in the Senate over the next ten months is truly astonishing. Soon after returning to Washington in October, he made an emotional appeal to the Senate to prevent exemption of ammunition sales from the Gun Control Act of 1968. Stony-faced Senators crushed his amendment 65 to 19. In November, Kennedy saw President Nixon skim the cream from his pet project—draft reform—by instituting the lottery system by Executive order. "Do you feel you've been taken to the cleaners on this?" Kennedy was asked by a reporter. He refused to comment.

Then came Kennedy's two amendments to the tax bill. The first went down to defeat by 63 to 16; the second, which Kennedy had actually pushed through the Senate in identical form in 1967 (it later died in the House), was turned down 52 to 24. In December, the National Aeronautics and Space Administration stunned the state of Massachusetts by announcing that it would close the $60 million research complex in Cambridge built by funds allocated to his state by President Kennedy in 1962. And the young Senator who was sent to Washington in 1962 because he could "do more for Massachusetts" was powerless to do anything to prevent this shutdown. In January, Kennedy's amendment to the Administration crime bill was overwhelmed 62 to 11. And in February, Kennedy, who almost never gets sick, came down with pneumonia.

In the new year, Kennedy tried a fresh tack. If his being counted out of the Presidential stakes had drastically curtailed the sort of influence he had enjoyed before, perhaps the new situation in which he found himself contained within it different opportunities—such as, the issue of the 18-year-old voter. Here, indeed, was an issue ready-made for Kennedy—or so it seemed to him at the time. Before Chappaquiddick, while still a likely Presidential nominee with a well-known appeal to young voters, any move by Kennedy to lower the voting age would have appeared self-serving and therefore doomed to defeat. But as a non-candidate with nothing to gain from young voters, it seemed a perfectly appropriate cause for him to champion. Accordingly, early in 1970, Kennedy circulated a memorandum among Democratic Senators urging them to join with him in pressing for a lowering of the voting age to 18. Some support developed. Then, just when it seemed as though this might be an idea whose time had come, Majority Leader Mansfield seized an opportunity when Kennedy was out of the country to introduce the measure under his own name, figuring that Kennedy's would only hinder its chances for passage. The measure virtually shot through the Senate, being passed by a vote of 64 to 17; shortly after, it was passed by the House and signed into law by President Nixon. A success in one respect, the bill's passage nevertheless represented yet another defeat for Kennedy, and a particularly serious one at that, because Mansfield's tactics demonstrated to all of Kennedy's colleagues that the majority leader still considered his name poison.

Some weeks later, when it developed that the liberals in the Senate were going to make a serious fight against President Nixon's Supreme Court nominee Clement Haynsworth, Kennedy, being one of the more liberal senior members of the Senate Judiciary Committee, seemed a good choice to lead the battle. But, because of his own entanglement with the courts of Massachusetts at that time, this plum fell to Birch Bayh of Indiana. Again, when Nixon's second choice for the Court, G. Harrold Carswell, was being considered, it was Kennedy who delivered one of the sharpest Senate-floor attacks against him, yet his eloquence fell on deaf ears. His comments were relegated in the next day's *New York Times* to paragraph nineteen in a story about the floor fight. Many newspapers ignored his speech altogether. Perhaps Kennedy's greatest frustration came a short while later when the Senate Interior and Insular Affairs Committee held hearings to study a recommendation to change the name of Cape Kennedy back to Cape Canaveral. Advocates of the name change insisted they intended no disrespect to the memory of the late President, nor to his surviving brother, but, all things considered, they would just as soon return the honor to Ponce de Leon, who named the cape "Canaveral" (or "Canebrake Cape") while he was blundering about Florida looking for the Fountain of Youth. The proponents of the name-change never managed to get their bill out of committee, but the fact that such a thing would even be attempted was a dire indication of Kennedy's standing.

If Kennedy seemed to have been stripped of personal power in the Senate, he had by no means lost that skill which he had acquired over seven years as a Senator and one year as majority whip in the esoteric cloakroom art sometimes referred to as wheeling and dealing but which might more accurately be described as legislative management—and which is, after all, the way things get done in Congress. Kennedy is uncommonly good at it. In fact, Mike Mansfield went so far as to tell me that Kennedy's effectiveness as whip may even have increased after Chappaquiddick. "After the accident," Mansfield remarked one day in the majority leader's office just off the Senate floor, "members did not go after him as hard as they did prior to that time when they considered him a prime political target because people thought he was running for President."

A fascinating illustration of Kennedy's effectiveness as a manager of legislation was the way in which he wheedled through the Senate an amendment (which bore a colleague's name) to the Hill-Burton Act, which allocated federal funds to the states for hospital construction. It is especially interesting that this success occurred just at the time when Kennedy was having such disastrous experiences with those other efforts which were undertaken in his own name.

As a member of the health subcommittee of the Labor and Public Welfare Committee (he has since become chairman of the subcommittee), Kennedy had long been nettled by the fact that under the antiquated Hill-Burton Act, which was adopted in 1946, Massachusetts, among other Northern states, was being shortchanged in the federal grants it received for hospital construction. Unfortunately, nothing could be done to amend the Act so long as Lister Hill, the aging Alabaman who co-authored the bill nearly a quarter century ago, remained chairman of the Labor and Public Welfare Committee. Hill had carefully devised the formula for fund allocation so that it would disproportionately benefit the rural South, including, of course, his home state, and he would simply not hear of any proposal to change it, no matter how loudly his Yankee colleagues might grouse about the shortage of hospital beds in their states. But Hill retired in 1968. The new chairman, advanced by the seniority system in the Senate, was Ralph Yarborough, the Texas liberal. Yarborough's accession to the chairmanship did not exactly open the floodgates to change, however, since it so happened that under the old formula Texas was receiving more money than any other state in the union. And Yarborough, then facing the toughest election of his career (he would soon be defeated), was not about to suddenly become loftily moral about plunging Texas' pitchfork into the federal pork barrel. Nevertheless, Yarborough had no personal stake in the original act, and therefore Kennedy saw a chance for change.

Kennedy surmised that if a formula for the more equitable distribution of federal funds were worked out to everyone's satisfaction, it would have to be a pretty elegant piece of higher math, taking into account not only the merits but the politics of the matter. It would have to accomplish the following:

1. Leave Texas the leading recipient so that Yarborough would lend his name and support to the amendment.
2. At the same time give Massachusetts and the other northern states a more fairly proportionate share of the funds.
3. Without significantly affecting factors 1 and 2, increase the benefits for a great enough number of states to secure the support of a majority of Senators so that the amendment would be adopted by the Senate.

Clearly, this was a job for a computer. Accordingly, as soon as Kennedy had lined up Jacob Javits, the New York Republican, to cosponsor the project in order to give it bipartisan backing, he arranged for Javits and himself to meet with statisticians of the Department of Health, Education and Welfare to explain the problem to them and to ask if they could work out the desired formula. Remarkably, the H.E.W. statisticians said they had no computer at their disposal, but they believed they could come up with the answer by employing a number of calculating machines. Kennedy and Javits told them to go to it, and to call as soon as they had a formula.

For several days the statisticians struggled with their figures. At first, under what seemed to be an ideal formula—one appropriating funds to states on the basis of giving equal weight to population, per capita income and need for health facilities (based on a standard H.E.W. yardstick) —Texas came out the top recipient and the northern states became gainers, too. But then it was shown that the total number of states getting more than they received under the old formula was only 22, and there would be 28 losers. Since this would spell certain doom in the Senate, this formula had to be scrapped. Going back to their calculating machines, the statisticians finally came up with the perfect solution: allocate 40 per cent of the Hill-Burton funds to states on the basis of population; another 40 per cent on the basis of per capita income squared; and 20 per cent on the basis of need—and you would wind up with Texas being the greatest beneficiary (score 1) ; Massachusetts, New York and several other Northern states making significant gains in the funds allocated to them (score 2) ; and 29 states receiving more money under the new formula than the old (bingo!) .

Not surprisingly, Yarborough was happy to lend his name to the new amendment and to introduce it on the Senate floor. When the roll was called—and this was the real testament to Kennedy—the amendment was adopted without a single opposing vote. Those who might have voted against it recognized that Kennedy had so effectively canvassed both the merits and the politics of the bill that opposition would be pointless. While the measure subsequently bogged down in a House-Senate Conference committee, which appointed a H.E.W. committee of experts to study the advisability of the new formula, and while the final outcome is still uncertain, there can be no question of the political skill with which Kennedy carried this piece of legislation through the Senate.

Such accomplishments, I imagined, must have done something to reassure Kennedy at least in regard to his professional competence during the year following the accident at Chappaquiddick; yet there could be no escaping the fact that his influence in the Senate had declined precipitously. He acknowledged the latter—rather tangentially, as is often his way—during the conversation we had while driving back to Boston from New Haven. I had asked how he felt he had fared in the Senate after the accident.

"I think there are times when certain issues have to be raised and confronted," he began. "Like a lot of basic civil liberties questions. I'm going to continue to raise these issues because I believe I'm fulfilling a responsibility to the Senate, to my own beliefs, and to my state by doing so. There are those who may say you've lost some impact, but in the long run if you continue to raise the issues you believe in, your colleagues will think more of you."

A few days later, as we were walking along the banks of the Charles River near his home in Boston, I remarked that one of his colleagues had told me that in order to reestablish himself in the Senate, Kennedy was going to have to "start all over again from scratch." Kennedy smiled. "I don't think you ever start from scratch with your concerns, or hopefully, with your knowledge of the institution or interest in the issues," he said.

Kennedy then went on to talk about his long association with and affection for the Senate. "I can remember," he said, "the first time I ever visited there. It was back in 1953 and I was a schoolboy. My brother John had just been elected to the Senate. I'd come down to visit him on the night train. Getting in early, I arrived at his office at about 7:30 in the morning. No one was there. So I sat down on my suitcase out in the hall. Next door was the office of the Vice President, and just then Nixon came along. He introduced himself and invited me into his office. It was the first time I'd ever met him. We had a pleasant talk, sparring about who got in first in the morning and that sort of thing. Later, my brother showed me all around the Senate. I was tremendously impressed."

Kennedy went on to say that he has felt at home in the Senate almost ever since. "I rarely take the Capitol subway —only when it's raining terrifically hard," he told me. "I like to walk whenever I can and go by where both Jack's office was and where Bobby's office was. I can remember different things Bobby said as I pass by the places where we stood and talked. When I go by the north entrance hall, I think of President Kennedy delivering his inaugural address there and I remember that was where the country honored him at the end.

"I have many associations there," he continued. "But beyond that, I feel the Senate is where the action is, where the great issues of war and peace, the issues of human rights and the problems of poverty are being debated. And, with certain important exceptions, you really *can* get a vote there on important matters. I would say the Senate is the greatest forum for change in our country and in the system. It's the forum that I very much want to be part of and have some influence with."

What was evident from such talk was that beaten and humiliated as Kennedy then was, forced as he was to contemplate the possibility of dropping out of public life altogether, he still loved the Senate—loved it as a young priest loves his church. And what he wanted most of all to do was simply to follow the advice of the fans he met on city streets throughout his state who called out to him, "Hang in there, Ted!" He wanted, quite desperately, I felt, to hang in there.

IX

HOW MANY VOTES CONSTITUTE FORGIVENESS?

BOSTON, MASSACHUSETTS—He figured, naturally enough, that the place for him to start rebuilding his influence—if, indeed, it could be done anywhere—was at home in Massachusetts. Clearly, Kennedy was not threatened with defeat in the Senatorial election of November, 1970, but the size of his plurality in an election that happened to fall just 15 months after the accident at Chappaquiddick was sure to be interpreted by his Senate colleagues, and by pundits and professional politicians around the country, too, as either a vote of confidence or a vote of little or no confidence. The question was: How much would be enough? Would a plurality of a quarter of a million votes constitute forgiveness? Or would it take a half-million? Or a million?

The answer lay in what an informal consensus of professional observers would determine as his handicap, based on all the built-in factors that he had working for and against him, and also how they would compare his performance with those of the other champions around the country, such as Muskie and Humphrey, who were also up for re-election that year.

For example, one knowledgeable local observer hazarded a guess that Kennedy would be doing well if he won by half a million votes. No one expected that he could possibly win by over a million votes, capturing 74 percent of the total as he had in his spectacular victory in 1964. That year, Kennedy had had a number of extraordinary factors working in his favor: an outpouring of sympathy as a result of his having lost his brother only a year before; the coattail effect of the Johnson landslide victory over Goldwater; and the absence of stiff competition due to a lackluster and poorly financed Republican opposing him. In 1970, in contrast, in place of sympathy there would be the specter of scandal. In addition, this was an off-year election so there would be no coattail effect; indeed, there was a possibility of backlash, owing to what his staff called "the 128 problem"—serious unemployment in the defense industry plants located along Route 128, which rings Boston and where people were saying, "If Kennedy had only kept his mouth shut about the war, we might still have our jobs." Finally, Kennedy's Republican opponent, Josiah Spaulding, was an engaging, hard-working and independently wealthy former state chairman of the Republican party. Even before securing the nomination, Spaulding had spent more money gearing up his effort than his predecessor in 1964 spent on the entire campaign. Spaulding's prospective budget was $1.5 million and if he came anywhere close to raising and spending such a sum of money, it could not help but significantly affect the November returns.

On the other hand, Kennedy continued to be something of a demigod in his home state. Massachusetts newspaper editors quite frequently received worshipful letters about him. To quote from a letter typical of this genre that *The Boston Herald-Traveler* published soon after Chappaquiddick: "Ted could push my 80-year old mother down on Boston Common, stomp my dog and spit on me. I would be so proud I would never wash again!" It would be easy to dismiss such sentiments as those of an isolated simple soul, but the belief that the Kennedys can do no wrong is remarkably widespread in Massachusetts. The respected Massachusetts Poll, conducted by the Becker Research Corporation for *The Boston Globe,* for example, showed that on the weekend following Kennedy's television speech about Chappaquiddick no fewer than 84 per cent of the voters in his state approved of the way he was handling his job as Senator. His approval rating slipped to 78 per cent two months later, but zoomed up to 87 per cent the following spring.

In any case, Kennedy was taking no chances. His campaign for re-election in 1970, which he frankly described as "a major effort," got underway in earnest as far back as January of that year, when Kennedy held a public hearing on the subject of "noise pollution" in East Boston at a junior high school located directly under the approach of the big jets thundering down to Logan airport. The meeting was so well-attended and so widely publicized that Kennedy decided to use the device of holding hearings on subjects of local concern again and again throughout the state

—on dangerous drugs in Winchester and Lynn, on postwar economic conversion in the electronics-industry centers of Framingham and Lexington, on federal aid to the fishing industry in the port cities of Gloucester and New Bedford, on the problems of the aging in Fall River, on insurance for policemen in Worcester and Boston, and on federal aid to secondary schools in Somerville, Arlington and Cambridge.

Meanwhile, Kennedy's campaign organization mounted a high-powered drive to register new Democratic voters. The idea was to do something to offset the customary "drop off" of about 300,000 voters in the state who could be counted on not to bother to register to vote in an off-year election. Young voters were to be a particular target of the registration drive, both because the young traditionally fail to register, and because a Becker poll in March, 1970 revealed that Kennedy continued to be far and away the most favored Presidential prospect among young people in Massachusetts. Kennedy's 27 per cent rating in a field of seven was a full nine percentage points ahead of his closest rival, Edmund Muskie.

The registration drive, headed by a fulltime professional and staffed by 35 regional coordinators, ultimately had a local chairman in every ward and precinct throughout the state marshalling an army of thousands of doorbell ringers and telephone callers. Well-financed, too, this effort became the biggest item, next to television advertising, in Kennedy's $1.2 million campaign budget.

As the registration drive got into full swing, Kennedy spent less and less time in Washington and stepped up his schedule of personal appearances throughout the state. "The people want to see him," I was told by David E.

Harrison, the tall, slim, young Democratic state chairman who was serving as one of Kennedy's three campaign managers. "They know he's had problems, so they want to see for themselves that he's still the same guy."

Kennedy began showing the voters what kind of a guy he was at clubhouse dinners and firemen's balls, on courthouse steps and in handshake hikes down Main Street. His speeches stressed what one of his lieutenants described as "the heritage theme"—that is, the not-so-subtle reminder that Ted Kennedy comes, in the words of one local wag, "from the people who brought you Jack and Bobby." I witnessed the heritage theme being put to work with striking success one day when Kennedy addressed the annual luncheon of the Democratic Women on Wheels of Massachusetts, Inc., a large group of politically active women who had gathered in the dining room of the cruise ship *Peter Stuyvesant,* which was tied up at a Boston pier. The pitch went like this: First, Kennedy blasted Nixon for appealing to base instincts with his Southern strategy. In contrast, said Kennedy, "You and I remember Democratic Administrations that appealed to the highest ideals of America." Next, he lit into Vice President Agnew for exploiting the division between young and old, following up this attack with the refrain, "I remember Democratic Administrations that tried to bring people together." Finally, he denounced the Republican leadership for abandoning the war on poverty, winding up with, "And I remember Democratic Administrations, my friends, that were devoting their energies to *helping* the poor." When he was finished, the women stood up and cheered. None of this rhetoric had much to do with the problems of Massachusetts, of course, but it most forcefully served to remind everyone present who the speaker was and to engender in them the sort of spine-tingling nostalgia that might well bring Kennedy voters to the polls in hordes.

By the time election day arrived, the registration effort had been an unqualified success. There had been a net "drop off" in registered voters throughout the state of only 80,000, which indicated that something like 220,000 voters who otherwise might not have registered had signed up. As for the election itself, Kennedy defeated Spaulding by a little more than half a million votes, winning 63 per cent of the total number of ballots cast, which was 11 percentage points off from his startling 1964 result. Muskie won exactly the same per cent of the vote in Maine as had Kennedy in Massachusetts, and that was a decline of four percentage points from Muskie's 1964 victory; Humphrey trailed by garnering 58 per cent of the vote in Minnesota, the same slice of the vote as he had captured in 1960.

Most observers considered Kennedy's margin of victory a little better than might have been expected, although certainly not spectacular. As Warren Weaver, Jr., *The New York Times* political analyst, commented in an article in *Esquire,* Kennedy's 63 per cent was "strong for an off year, but perhaps not all that remarkable for the last of the Kennedys, on his Massachusetts home ground, imploring the faithful to prove that he was not a political pariah." In any case, the consensus seemed to be that, all things considered, Kennedy had indeed won his vote of confidence. He had passed the point of having to worry about whether his "effectiveness is there." Resignation seemed out of the question. He was now a third-term Senator in good standing with his home-state constituency—if not, perhaps, with the nation as a whole.

And if not, perhaps, with his colleagues in the Senate, either. While concentrating his energies on the campaign in Massachusetts, Kennedy had neglected his duties as majority whip, and he would soon find himself having to pay a price for that vote of confidence in Massachusetts that he had not bargained on. During Kennedy's prolonged spring and summer absences from the Senate floor, his duties as whip had fallen to the third-ranking party official in the chamber, the secretary of the Democratic conference. Robert Byrd, the scrappy and conservative West Virginian who held this post, used the opportunity to ingratiate himself with his colleagues (always being sure. for example, to let them know when their votes were not vital on a certain measure so they could catch an early flight home) , and, in January, 1971, Byrd snatched the job of whip from. Kennedy by surprise, just as Kennedy had wrested it from Russell Long two years before.

This hurt, but the damage was minor. Recovering quickly, Kennedy went on to become chairman of a Senate subcommittee on health by persuading three more senior members in line for the job that he ought to have it. And with the passage of time Kennedy began to look upon his defeat as whip with relief. For now that he was no longer tied to the Senate as one of its functionaries, he was liberated from a confining solicitude toward senior members, and he could speak out with less fear of treading on venerable toes. Physically, too, Kennedy found himself liberated —free to travel around the country to touch base with old friends and to make politically fruitful trips to Israel and India. He found himself free enough and strong enough so that by late 1971 he could even make a five-state swing around the country, acting like a Presidential candidate, and return home perhaps a trifle unsure of the result, yet certainly far from disappointed. He would always bear the scars of Chappaquiddick, but at least now it was clear that the accident had not crippled him.

Part
THREE

AFTER BOBBY

X

'THIS WAS
BOBBY'S YEAR'

WASHINGTON, D.C.—When Ted Kennedy pulled up a chair in his Senate office beside the buff-colored couch where he likes to talk with reporters—serving cranberry juice and long, slender Philippine *cigarillos* *—I spied over his shoulder a painting of a mist-gray destroyer plunging through heavy seas. It was the *U.S.S. Joseph P. Kennedy, Jr.,* named for the Senator's oldest brother, who had died a war hero in 1944. Until June, 1968, the painting had hung in the office of Senator Robert Kennedy, who served as a seaman aboard the ship. The scene depicts *The Kennedy* pitching and drenched, as if she had just weathered a storm and now, for the first time, has burst out into the sun.

---

* Invariably an Alhambra Mahaba Regaliz.

Yet the sea still has a treacherous look. And from the motion of the water, and the direction of her brightly colored signal flags snapping in the wind, it appears that *The Kennedy* is in what sailors call a following sea—that is, with the wind and waves coming from astern, the vessel pulses forward through the water at an accelerated rate of speed and is at her most difficult to steer.

After the death of Robert Kennedy, Ted, who had always been outdistanced by the performance of his older brothers, suddenly found himself being thrust forward in political life at such a giddy speed that he had to fight for control. Although just one year over the constitutionally imposed age for the Presidency, he was boomed for his party's nomination. The opinion polls indicated that he alone could save the Democrats from defeat. Mayors of great cities, state governors, even the most likely nominee of the party, Hubert Humphrey, importuned him to lend his name to the ticket.

On at least one occasion, he was tempted. That was during the Democratic nominating convention three months after his brother's death when Mayor Richard J. Daley of Chicago, one of the key power brokers, told him the nomination was his for the asking. Kennedy sought advice: "Daley says we can just *have* it," he told a friend.

Yet he decided not to ask. Kennedy felt himself too young, too inexperienced and too stricken with grief to reach for the prize. Furthermore, it seemed simply wrong to him that he should inherit, as if in a feudal society, the political position his brother Robert had attained.

The "Draft Kennedy" movement he resisted had been born in a freakish encounter only minutes after Robert Kennedy's death. Ted Kennedy had spent the evening of

June 4, 1968—the night the returns from the California Presidential primary election were being counted—at a celebration in a San Francisco hotel much like the one his older brother was attending that night at the Ambassador Hotel in Los Angeles, four hundred miles to the south. Toward eleven o'clock, when the defeat of Eugene McCarthy seemed apparent, Kennedy returned to his room at the Fairmont Hotel in downtown San Francisco with his administrative assistant, David Burke. As soon as the two men entered Kennedy's room, one of them flicked on a television set to catch the latest news.

The news program they happened to tune in showed a scene of riotous confusion. Thinking the telecast was originating at the hotel they had just left, Burke remarked to Kennedy with relief, "We're lucky we got out of there." Just then the picture focused on Stephen Smith, Kennedy's brother-in-law, at a speaker's platform asking in a strained voice for a doctor. Kennedy and Burke, standing in front of the television set, bent forward with curiosity. They recognized at once that they were watching the scene at the Ambassador Hotel in Los Angeles, and that something strange had happened. The picture on the screen shifted to the floor of the ballroom where a small knot of people appeared seized with frenzy. Then came screams and shouts. An agonized voice cried: "No, God, no! It's happened again!" And then a television reporter, his voice breaking with shock and alarm, said Robert Kennedy had been shot.

Ted Kennedy stared at the screen for a few moments without expression, and without seeming to move a muscle. Then he said to Burke in a low voice, "Let's get out of here."

The two men rode together in a taxi to the airport, flew to Los Angeles in a hastily-requisitioned Air Force jet and proceeded by helicopter to the Hospital of the Good Samaritan. "All that time he didn't say anything," Burke later recalled. "That was the thing about it. He set his jaw and he said nothing. He just didn't say anything at all."

He was the last of the circle of intimates to arrive. The others—Stephen Smith, Ethel Kennedy and other members of the Kennedy family, as well as Theodore Sorensen, Pierre Salinger, David Hackett, Andy Williams, Edwin Guthman, were already at the hospital. Ted Kennedy went straight to his brother's bedside and learned at once that he was dying. One bullet had caused only a superficial cut in his shoulder but another had inflicted a mortal wound in his brain.

Surgery was begun at 2:30 A.M. and continued for more than three hours. When it was over, Robert Kennedy's press secretary announced that the next "twelve to thirty-six hours will be a very critical period." But Ted Kennedy knew better. Almost as soon as there was light in the sky the next morning, he and Stephen Smith began to make arrangements for the funeral. Later in the day, Kennedy and Burke visited a mortuary to select a casket. Returning to the hospital, Kennedy came up to old friends of his brother and said, "Do you want to go in and see him? It's only a matter of time."

In the early morning hours of June 6th, the end came. Ted was at his brother's bedside, along with a priest, his brother's wife Ethel, his two sisters Jean and Patricia, Jacqueline Kennedy and Stephen Smith. Minutes afterward, a strange, awkward and significant meeting took place.

Allard K. Lowenstein, the articulate young political activist who had organized the "dump Johnson" campaign, had come to the hospital, as had many others, to pay his respects. Lowenstein venerated, perhaps even worshipped, Robert Kennedy. Yet the year before when Lowenstein had begged him to wage a campaign in the state primaries against Lyndon Johnson, Kennedy had turned him down. So Lowenstein had gone to Eugene McCarthy, finding in him a candidate willing to fight. That put Lowenstein in the McCarthy camp, and when Robert Kennedy belatedly entered the lists in March, 1968, Lowenstein felt torn but nevertheless honor-bound to stick with McCarthy even though his heart was with Kennedy.

Bitterness developed between the two camps after President Johnson announced that he would not stand for re-election, and McCarthy and Kennedy turned against each other. Through the succeeding primaries Lowenstein's position became increasingly difficult, and by the time he arrived at the Hospital of the Good Samaritan in Los Angeles he did not know how he would be received and was even fearful that in their grief some Kennedy supporters there might actually abuse him. Accordingly, shortly after Lowenstein heard the announcement that Robert Kennedy was dead, he decided to slip away alone. In the hallway outside the waiting room he pushed an elevator button and when a door opened he stepped on an elevator—realizing when it was too late to back off that he had blundered onto the elevator in which Ted Kennedy and John Tunney, Ted's closest personal friend, were accompanying the sheet-wrapped body of Robert Kennedy on the trip to the autopsy room in the basement of the hospital.

"I felt I shouldn't be there," Lowenstein recalls, "but

there was no way I could get off, nothing I could do." In the basement, the body was wheeled off and the passengers followed. Lowenstein recalls being "emotionally out of control" and saying "a lot of presumptuous things." One of the things he said to Kennedy was, "Now that Bobby's gone, you're all we've got." Then Lowenstein beseeched Kennedy to "take the leadership."

Kennedy thanked Lowenstein "with great politeness," embraced him and stated, according to Lowenstein, that "he would carry on." Looking back on those awkward moments which suddenly led to "a very moving and memorable experience," Lowenstein says he believes that that was the juncture at which Ted Kennedy decided to run for President. He is probably wrong. The thought may have flashed through Kennedy's mind, but he certainly did not come to a final decision. Perhaps when he told Lowenstein he would "carry on" he simply meant that he would not drop out of political life. In any case, this seems to have been the moment at which the "Draft Kennedy" movement was born, for it was Lowenstein who was to become the unsanctioned, undercover organizer of the effort to induce Kennedy to lend his name to the ticket at the nominating convention in Chicago three months later.

Kennedy's reasons for saying no to the draft—via telephone calls to Mayor Daley and others in Chicago from Hyannis Port, where he later secluded himself—were, as previously stated, several in number. One of his principal reasons, however, was particularly revealing. "This was Bobby's year," he told a friend, explaining why he had finally decided against encouraging or submitting to a draft. The remark alludes to an interesting fact about the relationships in the Kennedy family; namely, that although the brothers were competitive with each other, they also accepted their places in a rigid hierarchy.

The elder's "rightful" place always was on top. This meant Ted could compete against Bobby vigorously, but he could not triumph over his older brother without feeling guilt for having upset the hierarchy, and when this situation arose Ted would immediately set about to restore Bobby's position of supremacy by making disparaging jokes about himself or otherwise permitting Bobby to get on top again. When Bobby was killed, Ted felt not just grief but guilt—guilt for having triumphed over (by surviving) his older brother, a guilt that could not be assuaged by putting Bobby back up where he had been. The fact that Ted was then offered the prize his brother was seeking, and been cheated of by an assassin, only compounded his guilt feelings. And thus, the notion of accepting a draft for the Presidential nomination seemed to Ted Kennedy an unconscionable thing to do. 1968 was, as he said, "Bobby's year."

The competitive side of the relationship between the Kennedys had always been much easier to see than the hierarchical one. Many friends and associates described the former; few seemed aware of the latter. Senator Gaylord Nelson of Wisconsin, for example, sat between the two brothers on the Labor and Public Welfare committee and therefore caught a good deal of the byplay between them. "They were always making humorous remarks to each other," Nelson recalls, "and the remarks were always at each other's expense. At one meeting of the committee, I remember, Bobby introduced a bill and some substantive questions were asked. Bobby wasn't too well prepared and couldn't answer the questions. Everyone was a little embarrassed for him. Then Ted threw his hands up in mock despair and said in a loud, disapproving voice, 'Well, that's par for the course!' It broke everybody up, but you knew he was having fun teasing his brother."

And Ted's friend Senator Birch Bayh of Indiana recalls having been amazed on several occasions by the way the Kennedy brothers practiced one-upmanship. "The greatest gleam I ever saw in Ted's eye," Bayh recalls, "was one day in the summer of 1965 when he took Jack's old sailboat and beat Bobby in a race when Bobby had the latest sort of boat with all the newest equipment."

Behind this façade of free-swinging competition, however, was the reality of the hierarchy. One of the few outsiders who perceived this aspect of the brothers' relationship recalls: "Bobby followed that older brother thing to the hilt. Ted doesn't know I know this, but *he* wanted to climb Mt. Kennedy, too, after the peak had been named for Jack. He was willing to let Bobby carry the flag, but he felt he should be able to make the climb. He had to wait six or eight months, however, for his back to mend. Bobby said, '*Hell,* I'm not waiting for *him.*' So he climbed Mt. Kennedy and left Ted in the hospital."

In 1966, *Newsweek* was preparing a long story about the two Kennedy brothers then serving in the Senate. When the magazine's Washington bureau asked the Kennedys to pose together for a cover picture on the steps of the Capitol, Bobby sent Ted out to meet the photographer, explaining haughtily that *he* did not have time for such trivia, and that a stock photograph of him could be mechanically pasted in beside Ted: it must, he insisted, show him standing slightly higher than Ted. *Newsweek* agreed. So did

Ted, who had learned to accept this sort of treatment from his brother.

Naturally, no hint of such goings-on crept into the eulogy of Bobby that Ted delivered in Saint Patrick's Cathedral in New York City. Yet this dominant psychological fact of their relationship was what made it finally impossible for Ted to take over his brother's Presidential campaign.

When Kennedy rejected the draft, he was not, as some observers speculated at the time, preparing to drop out of public life. A few close friends, even one archbishop, had counseled precisely that, both for his safety and for the sake of his brothers' families. They urged him to do what Lincoln's only surviving son, Robert Todd, had done after being mentioned for the Presidency in the 1880s—retire to the relative obscurity of a good law practice.

Kennedy actually gave this course sober consideration. And he frankly told friends and a few reporters that he had decided not to appear in motorcades during the campaign—for security reasons. But it soon became apparent to him and to those around him that far from frightening him off, the killing of two of his brothers had only deepened his commitment to public life. 1968 was "Bobby's year," but there would be other years, and he would simply take his chances. At Worcester, Massachusetts, in the course of the first speech he delivered after the assassination, he said: "There is no safety in hiding. Not for me; not for any of us here today; and not for our children, who will inherit the world we make for them . . . Like my brothers before me, I pick up a fallen standard. . . ."

XI

TED GETS CRACKING

WASHINGTON, D.C.—No sooner was the election done with and Richard Nixon named the victor, than the press was filled with speculation about Kennedy's running against him in 1972. Rarely if ever had there been such excited attention devoted to the man a President-elect might have to face for re-election even before he himself was inaugurated.

As this discussion was reaching a crescendo, Kennedy startled the country by running for and winning the unlikely post of majority whip—the Senate functionary who assists the majority leader, and a job of such mean order that one senior Senator whose vote Kennedy had solicited blurted out a remark indicating that he did not even know who the then-present whip was.

134

Kennedy's telephone conversation with this particular patriarch from the Deep South is reliably reported to have gone like this:

KENNEDY: (*Reaching the Senator at his farm*) Good morning, Senator. This is Ted Kennedy calling from Washington. I'm calling to let you know that I've decided to run for majority whip.

PATRIARCH: I don't wanna buy no cattle today.

KENNEDY: What's that?

PATRIARCH: I said I'm *not* buyin' *no* cattle today.

KENNEDY: Senator, it's Ted *Kennedy* in *Washington*.

PATRIARCH: Who?

KENNEDY: Ted Kennedy.

PATRIARCH: Kinndy! Wha'chew want, Kinndy?

KENNEDY: I'm calling to say that I'm running for whip of the Senate. I wanted to let you know that's what I've decided to do.

PATRIARCH: That job ain't vacant.

KENNEDY: I know. But I want to run anyway.

PATRIARCH: Wha'chew wanna take Bobby Byrd's job fo?

KENNEDY: Bobby Byrd isn't whip. I'm running against Russell Long.

PATRIARCH: Wha'chew wanna run against Russell Long fo?

KENNEDY: I think I should. I'm calling to solicit your vote, Senator.

PATRIARCH: Shee-it.

This patriarch from the South was not alone in his bewilderment. The press and professional politicians around the country were left scratching their heads trying to figure out why the most glamorous public figure in the United States suddenly aspired to carry a water bucket. Was this a case of a young man on the way down? Or was there some deucedly clever motive behind it?

Some Washington observers came forward with the theory that Kennedy's decision to run for whip was part of a carefully devised plan to build a power base from which to launch the second attempt at Restoration. Exchanging knowing glances, these observers recalled that Hubert Humphrey had been whip at the time of his nomination for Vice President in 1964.

But the power-base theory stumbled over the fact that majority whip—despite the colorful English nomenclature —is anything but ringmaster of the Senate. That role is played by Mike Mansfield, the majority leader, who, as chairman of all of the Senate's internal Democratic party committees, and who is empowered with authority to appoint new members to them, is sometimes referred to, with only slight exaggeration, as potentially the second most powerful man in the country. The whip exists merely to do the majority leader's bidding—counting noses, bargaining for votes, excusing members from roll calls when their votes are not essential, and so forth. In terms of political power, therefore, it was Mike Mansfield who cracked the whip, and when he did, it would be Ted Kennedy's job to get cracking.

To be sure, the whip is also privy to deals and compromises, and has no end of opportunity to engage in cloakroom politicking. Yet no degree of coziness with any number of U.S. Senators is likely to blossom into a Presidential nomination. The power brokers at a Democratic nominating convention are the big-city mayors, patronage-rich state governors and minority-group and union leaders—which is precisely why Kennedy's two older brothers could afford to neglect the Senate when seriously contending for the nomination. For a man with his eyes on the White House, majority whip was about as imposing a "power base" as town crier of Gloucester, Massachusetts.

A second group of observers argued that Kennedy sought the whip's job as a platform from which to address the national audience. This theory flew in the face of the fact that being whip actually restricted his freedom to speak. It meant, for example, that he would have to devote several hours a day to being on the Senate floor, where TV cameras and microphones are barred and where he would be covered by relatively low-echelon reporters as opposed to the elite corps of the press who would follow him if he ventured out on the hustings. Being whip also meant that Kennedy had to turn down almost weekly invitations to speak out on foreign affairs on national television programs such as "Meet the Press" and "Face the Nation" in order not to risk upstaging his majority leader, whose major interest had long centered in this field. Moreover, even if a certain prominence *were* attached to being whip, Kennedy scarcely needed it; he commanded national attention just by being a Kennedy.

His real motive in going after the job was doubtless a compound of many things; motives always are. One important reason was that Kennedy felt that by becoming a member of the Senate leadership he would be perceived as having a "legitimate" interest in issues for their own sake, and thus not always arouse speculation that his every action was motivated by designs on the White House.

Chance provided another reason. Kennedy spent a brief

post-Christmas holiday with his family and a few close friends at the Sun Valley Lodge, an exclusive ski resort in the Sawtooth Mountains of Idaho. Arriving at the lodge, he discovered that his ski boots were missing from his luggage. Thus, while others in the party tramped off to the slope, Kennedy remained in his suite, telephoning the various airline baggage depots along his route to Sun Valley. The boots could not be located immediately, and, being of a restless nature, Kennedy made a few calls to friends and Senate colleagues.

In the course of one conversation, he learned that Senator Edmund Muskie had decided to abandon his effort to unseat Russell Long as majority whip. Then someone suggested that Kennedy run against Long. He began to alternate a second round of calls to baggage depots around the country with calls to further discuss the situation in the Senate. By the time his ski boots were found and delivered to Sun Valley, Kennedy had little use for them. He was running for whip.

The fundamental reason for Kennedy's decision, however, was psychological. In seeking this conspicuously unglamorous, workhorse-type assignment Kennedy was acting out the self-imposed rite of initiation that is a motif of his life and career. Call it the son-of-the-prominent-man complex, the scion's syndrome. The fact is that Edward Moore Kennedy desperately wants to prove that he is not coasting on his family reputation but has earned his stripes the hard way; that he could make it (in the idiom of his debate with Edward McCormick when he first ran for the Senate) even if his name *were* just Edward Moore.

It was this compulsion that led Kennedy to serve his military duty as an enlisted man rather than as an officer, and to slog around in the Army instead of joining the Navy, in which his brothers had distinguished themselves. It was also what prompted him to announce to friends during the 1960 Presidential campaign—in which he rather ineffectually managed 13 Western states—that if his brother lost the election and returned to the Senate he would move to the West and establish an independent political base there for himself.

Occasionally, through awkwardness or innocence, Kennedy's rugged determination to take the steepest path up the mountain seemed to demonstrate precisely the reverse of what he intended, and his rapid ascent looked to others as the result of pull, not push. In 1962, for instance, discounting the advice of those who urged him to run for the House of Representatives, Kennedy decided to try instead for the Senate, naively believing that his conquest of the entire state of Massachusetts, as opposed to just one of its congressional districts, would be seen as a triumph of his heaving at his own bootstraps.

As it turned out, however, the caper branded him spoiled and privileged rather than bold and self-reliant, since he swept to a thumping victory in the wake of disclosures about his lack of previous experience in elective office and suspension from Harvard, which, for anyone except a President's brother, would almost certainly have proved disastrous at the polls. Yet patiently, diligently, ploddingly working in the Senate year after year, Kennedy lived down his reputation as a pampered kid brother and came to be known and respected for his earnestness and dedication.

Not everyone was quite so forgiving, of course. Soon after the election of President Nixon in 1968, when some wit sent William F. Buckley, Jr. an "E.M.K. in 72" button, Buckley erupted in his syndicated newspaper column: "Really, the dynastic assertiveness of the Kennedys is a wonder of the world." He then foamed on about "arrant opportunism." There are also a few Senators who harbor gripes against Kennedy. "He plays everything too close to the chest," says a colleague who was once inconvenienced when Kennedy told him less than the whole truth involving a matter of personal and political delicacy. But, by and large, even Kennedy's ideological opponents now honor him for his seriousness of purpose and hard work.

If the country as a whole forgot the criticism heaped upon him for his too-easy victory in 1962, however, Kennedy did not. That hit him where he lived. And so, at Sun Valley, when he saw an opportunity to again go over an obstacle course, to rub out his most-recent unwanted image as the multi-millionaire who looks smashing on the slopes in a white wool cable-stitched sweater, and show himself instead the tough work-a-day legislator ready and willing to struggle with all the grubby little details of getting some worthwhile law on the books, he jumped at the chance.

XII

A PLUGGER'S PROGRESS

WASHINGTON, D.C.—Two weeks after his election as whip, I wangled * a meeting with Kennedy in his quarters in the Old Senate Office Building to find out how he was adjusting to this new loss of a brother and to discover, if I could, what plans he was making for the future. Although he did tell me a number of interesting things about the Senate, this interview turned out to be difficult in one respect: on several occasions when I asked Kennedy what he had accomplished in the Senate and what he thought could be done there, he started talking about Bobby's achievements and Bobby's expectations. Once, when he mentioned his brother, he choked and looked

---

* See Preface.

away from me. When he returned his gaze, his eyes were filled with tears. Bobby had been dead for six months.

Before reporting that interview, which included a rather technical discussion about the Senate, I will sketch in some background by setting down a few words about that curious, and surprisingly little-understood institution, the United States Senate. And then a few words about Kennedy's relationship with it.

To begin with, in practice, the Senate bears little resemblance to the democratic institution it is pictured as in the general run of high school and even college textbooks. True enough, its actions are governed by voting and the rule of the majority, yet ever since the election of 1920, a small and extremely conservative band of senators, mostly from the South—they are known in Washington as "the Club"—has enjoyed almost complete control over which matters shall and which shall not be brought to a vote. Thus, they have run the Senate not according to the wishes of the majority of its members, but according to the dictates of their own very narrow views and concerns.

The Club maintains its control by taking advantage of the fact that the Senate is divided into 16 "little senates" known as committees. No matter may be placed on the floor of the Senate for discussion and action until it has first been considered by the appropriate one of these committees. And since the committees have the power to refuse to "report out" matters for consideration by the Senate as a whole, they may exercise a sort of veto-in-advance over the agenda, and thus thwart the will of the majority.

In order to dominate the Senate, the Club does not even need to control all 16 of its committees. Most of the committees, like the District of Columbia Committee and the

Labor and Public Welfare Committee deal with matters that are not controversial nor of any great importance in terms of national politics: these are known as "Orphan Annies," because most members have no interest in serving on them. Four of the 16 committees, however, are the powerhouses—Appropriations, Finance, Armed Services, and Foreign Relations—because they concern themselves with substantial and controversial matters like money, military power and foreign policy. Most members, naturally, are eager to serve on these committees. But the Club manages to control the powerhouses by keeping its members on them in the majority (and in the chairmanships, too) and by "packing" the liberals on the undesirable Orphan Annies.

The Club's ability to control which members will serve on which committees is based on its domination of the party organs that have the power of committee assignment. These bodies are the Steering Committee, in the case of the Democrats; and the Committee on Committees for the Republicans. Thus, for example, at the commencement of the session in which Kennedy was elected whip, the Democratic Steering Committee assigned three newly elected liberals—Harold Hughes of Iowa, Alan Cranston of California, and Thomas Eagleton of Missouri—to the Labor and Public Welfare Committee, an Orphan Annie where their votes would make little difference, while, at the same time, it passed over the liberal Birch Bayh in an appointment to the important Appropriations Committee, although Bayh was entitled to it by seniority, naming instead Joseph Montoya of New Mexico, a conservative. (The seniority system is only a custom, occasionally violated in the committee assignments of junior senators, more strictly observed within the committees in the selection of chairmen.) Barry Goldwater, also a staunch conservative, was appointed to Armed Services; other conservatives wound up on the Finance Committee—and so on.

How had Kennedy been treated by the Club? And how has he dealt with it? Being a liberal, of course, Kennedy was not appointed to any of the most important committees when he arrived in the Senate in 1962, but, as luck would have it, he did not fare too badly. That year both he and his friend Birch Bayh were appointed to the Judiciary Committee, which, while it is by no means one of the powerhouses, is not a limbo for a Northern liberal either, since it deals with civil rights legislation, gun control bills, and has, as we shall see, still other interesting potentialities. Kennedy and Bayh were not given such a good assignment as this because the Club deemed them trustworthy, but only because the Club was bent on punishing Quentin Burdick of North Dakota, who had long requested a seat on the Judiciary Committee, who deserved it by right of seniority, but who had opposed the Club by joining in an unsuccessful effort to curb the practice of filibuster. So when two vacancies on the Judiciary Committee occurred, Kennedy and Bayh were appointed to fill them to keep Burdick out. The lesson, of course, was not lost on the two young freshmen who became the beneficiaries of the punishment inflicted on a senior colleague.

Kennedy's other committee assignment (every Senator serves on at least two committees) was Labor and Public Welfare, which, as previously noted, is a kind of detention home for liberals—the liberals control it, but there is not much they can do with it. (Bobby Kennedy naturally wound up there with him.)

Once given his committee assignments, Kennedy had to watch his step. For example, if he should incur the displeasure of the Club, he could be "bumped"—removed from one or both of the committees on which he served, thus forfeiting all seniority. One of the more scandalous cases of bumping in recent years was the removal of the New York liberal Republican Jacob Javits from the Appropriations Committee, a heavy-handed gesture intended both as a reprimand to Javits and as a means of preventing a liberal from building up seniority on an important committee. "It is strangely anomalous," Javits complained on the Senate floor, "that when, finally, a member from New York—the financial center of the country . . . is placed on the Appropriations Committee, this unfortunate displacement occurs." But, of course, he and his friends were powerless to do anything except complain.

But Kennedy had to do more than just watch his step so as not to be pushed backward. If he ever hoped to achieve anything in the Senate he would have to ingratiate himself with his colleagues—especially the members of the Club. A challenging opportunity soon came along when Kennedy saw an opening on the Judiciary Committee that intrigued him—the vacant chairmanship of a subcommittee called the subcommittee on refugees and escapees from Communism. Kennedy foresaw that this subcommittee had a potentially powerful mandate; he decided he wanted the job. To get it he would have to be appointed by the chairman of the Judiciary Committee, Senator James O. Eastland of Mississippi, a heavy-set, jowly, plantation owner who happened to be a potent member of the Club, and who was a tireless defender of blacks against the threat of the right to vote, a superhawk on the war, an economic conservative, a man whose interests were primarily rural, and thus about as ideologically remote from Kennedy as one could get.

Kennedy set about to court Eastland. Whenever he could, he flattered him by asking for his advice. Invariably, Kennedy called him "Sir" or "Senator," and sprang to his feet in the Senate cloakroom when Eastland approached. Ted Kennedy, of course, has a special gift for getting along with older men. Having grown up at the bottom of the hierarchy of the Kennedy family, he learned at an early age that while he could not outdo his older brothers by being smarter or more experienced than they, he could frequently get what he wanted just by being amusing or charming. These tactics proved eminently transferable to the United States Senate. Another young member of the Senate told me of Kennedy's winning ways with admiration in his voice. "Ted knows very well," he said, "that many older people are really willing to bestow all sorts of beneficence on younger people. It makes them feel good to do it, but you have to be extremely careful that you handle the situations in which you ask for something in a delicate way. Ted's a master of that."

He *must* be a master, I thought to myself one day when I discovered how close a relationship Kennedy had managed to develop with Eastland. I had just visited Eastland to see what I could learn about how he and Kennedy got along, and had been nicely stymied. Upon hearing that I represented *The New York Times,* Eastland became mischievous. He propped his feet on his desk directly between the two of us so that I could not see his face. Everytime I shifted my position, Eastland moved his feet to block my view. Nor did he reveal much verbally in the course of the interview. What was revealing, however, was that when I strolled into Kennedy's office a few minutes later, I was told that Eastland had called and reported to Kennedy all of the questions I had asked him. Eastland, it seemed, was trying to curry favor with Kennedy!

Kennedy not only got the chairmanship of the subcommittee he had asked Eastland for, but also persuaded the old patriarch to let him drop the words "from Communism" from the committee's title, and to authorize the committee to look into the refugee situation in South Vietnam (where there may have been a few refugees and escapees from the Communist North, but a great many more displaced by the military rampages of the United States and its Saigon ally).

Later, Kennedy went to Eastland once more, and this time said he would like to take his subcommittee to Vietnam to observe the plight of the refugees at first hand. Eastland had to approve the trip itself, and also Kennedy's request to take along four assistants with "the privileges of the Senate,"—that is, with access to government transportation, lodging and so forth. In addition, since Kennedy wanted to visit Vietnamese hospitals, he decided it would be a good idea to take a physician with him, too. In due course, Eastland granted all of these requests, to any one of which he could have said no. While Kennedy could have traveled to Vietnam on his own, as many other members of Congress had done, he would have had to dispense with expert witnesses and the authority to investigate: his trip would have been much less effective.

Operating patiently and humbly within the system—as a "Senate man" some say—Kennedy naturally has been criticized for being too cautious, too orthodox, too much the operator, too little the impassioned champion. This last charge is heard especially from those devotees of "risk politics" who came to idolize Robert Kennedy only in the last three months of his life.

Indeed, this is a criticism that has been leveled at each of the Kennedy brothers in turn. John Kennedy was at one time characterized as a cagey shifter with every political zephyr, morally vacuous, "a Democratic Nixon." Bobby was called a tough, cynical and ruthless operator.

There is, it seems, a strong streak of romanticism in the American voters' psyche—curiously nettled by cool Kennedy pragmatism—which longs for boldness, which refuses to recognize the practical and moral complexities of political life (while recognizing them elsewhere), and which prizes above all else among actors on the national stage the hubris of telling it like it is, socking it to 'em, standing up and being counted for Truth and Justice regardless of the consequences, and regardless, too, of whether or not Truth and Justice are ultimately served.

Due to an odd development with an ironical twist to it, some of this—what might be called kamikaze charisma—did rub off on Kennedy as a result of the contest for majority whip. By the time he had publicly announced his candidacy, his chances of defeating Russell Long were already very good, and Kennedy knew it. But a leading member of the Capitol Hill press corps misjudged the odds and reported in *The New York Times* that Kennedy "was given little or no chance of unseating Senator Long" and that Long had received news of the challenge in "good humor."

With this, a thrill ran up the spines of the devotees of risk politics. "At last," one young risk politico in the House chirped, "Kennedy has undertaken something which is not guaranteed in advance."

148

Little did he know. Other Washington reporters had calculated the odds more accurately. Joseph R. L. Sterne of *The Baltimore Sun* wrote the day after Kennedy said he was running that the contest was going to be "a close one." And Mary McGrory, the Washington columnist, added the following day that Kennedy's chances were "excellent." Their more influential colleague, however, continued to regard Kennedy's effort as a long shot and naturally, when Kennedy finally won, was stuck with interpreting the victory as a daring gamble brilliantly executed in defiance of all the rules.

Of such stuff legends are made.

But diving his Zero down the stack of an enemy dreadnought is hardly Ted Kennedy's style. A story illustrative of his characteristic prudence in political affairs was told to me by Kennedy's administrative assistant, David Burke, who accompaned him on the subcommittee trip to South Vietnam to study the refugee situation. Mindful of the delicacy of his position in the Senate, and of his almost complete dependence on Eastland, Kennedy proceeded with care and caution. At one point during the tour, Kennedy and Burke inspected an artillery base near Dong-tam in the Mekong Delta that was engaged in H. & I. (harassment and interdiction) fire—random shelling at night of "suspected areas" which, according to U.S. military doctrine, kept the enemy on the run. Concerned that H. & I. fire might also be taking a toll among Vietnamese civilians and producing refugees, Kennedy asked the American base commander if anyone lived in the areas then under bombardment.

The commander showed him a big map indicating that no one lived within his firing range. Kennedy studied the map for a few minutes, then pointed out that it had been made by the French nine years ago—not exactly a reliable demographic check on a population unsettled by war. The commander cleared his throat and said that, in addition to the map check, every morning at eight o'clock he notified the local South Vietnamese province chief of the coordinates where the fire that night would strike. The province chief then checked down through his village chiefs to learn whether or not the designated area was clear of civilians, after which he reported back to the American commander by six o'clock in the evening. Firing commenced at eight o'clock.

"Did you tell the province chief where you are going to direct fire tonight?" Kennedy asked. "Yes, sir," said the commander. "And has the province chief called back?" The commander said he expected to hear from him shortly.

Kennedy and Burke then left the Cantho to look up the province chief. When they had located him, Kennedy asked if he knew where the H. & I. fire from the artillery base at Dong-tam was to be directed that night. The chief gave a knowing smile and shrugged his shoulders. Obviously, his regular "all clear" reports to the American commander were fiction; he never checked anything.

A few days later, Kennedy and Burke were on their way home. In Saigon, they happened to stop in at "Pentagon East," the military headquarters where V.I.P.'s are briefed on their arrival. Not realizing that Kennedy was on the point of departing rather than just off the plane from home, an unwary American colonel took the occasion to explain to the Senator the marvel of humane and scientific engineering that H. & I. fire is. Kennedy flew into a rage.

Back in Washington, he reported the incident to the Department of Defense and even brought it up during an hour-and-a-half interview with President Johnson. Yet he called no press conferences, nor did he explode in indignation about it on the Senate floor. "Because," Burke explained, "Kennedy knew he could not change the way the war was being fought. What he could do, however, was affect the way the Vietnamese government was treating its refugees once they had become casualties or displaced persons. And he accomplished that. He got an AID refugee program going, and he got five new hospitals for civilians built.

"He approached the war in Vietnam," Burke continued, "just as he approaches everything, asking first: how can I be effective? He isn't interested in winning accolades for taking 'righteous' positions. He wants results. It isn't that he lacks passion, you see, but that he passionately wants to be effective."

The story accurately portrays Kennedy's thinking and political technique, and yet Burke need not have been so modest about the larger consequences of what Kennedy was doing. He could indeed affect the way the war was being fought. For by focusing his attention on the seemingly peripheral problem of refugees, Kennedy was actually bringing to light an issue that went straight to the heart of American policy in Vietnam.

Many opponents of the war, for example, were willing to concede at that time that the United States' goal of keeping South Vietnam within the Western alliance was a reasonable one, if it could be achieved without undue violence. And, by the same token, a good many supporters of the war would seriously question the wisdom of waging it if they could be persuaded that hundreds of thousands, perhaps even millions, of individuals were being destroyed, maimed and displaced in order to keep this sliver of a remote half-nation within the Western sphere of influence. In short, the fundamental question about the war was becoming, as Eugene McCarthy was later to articulate it, one of proportion. And what Kennedy was doing with his subcommittee was counting the human cost of the execution of American policy—in terms of the number of children orphaned, families rendered homeless, even the number of arms and legs severed—in order to provide a rational basis for men of conscience to determine whether that cost was proportionate or disproportionate to the need of the policy in the first place.

During the summer and fall of 1967, Kennedy held hearings with the subcommittee and elicited some horrifying testimony from American doctors who had served in Vietnamese hospitals. One of the physicians, for example, testified as he showed slides: "This child was eight years old when this picture was taken . . . This is his hand. This is a napalm burn. This is his burn. It (his hand) is completely functionless. It is a club. This is after the first set of procedures some three months afterwards. He is not pretty but he can close his mouth and eyes."

Another doctor came up with equally horrifying statistics:

> DR. [ALFRED] SWANSON: They mentioned 35,000 amputations in this country (South Vietnam) . We had 20,000 in the whole of World War II U.S. forces, 20,000. They have had 35,000.
>
> SEN. KENNEDY: Could we ask one thing. That figure is extraordinary. We had 25,000 individuals who lost arms or legs in World War II?

DR. SWANSON: It is estimated 20,000.
SEN. KENNEDY: It is estimated 20,000. And *they*—
DR. SWANSON: Their estimate is 35,000 total war.
That is total war.

A third physician expressed his outrage that the richest
and mightiest nation in the world boasted of fighting for
the freedom of an impoverished peasant land while, in fact,
the Americans there demonstrated a fundamental contempt for that country's populace. "It is an unpleasant
truth," this doctor said, "that the hospitals in I Corp—
Quang Ngai, Quang Tri, Tam Ky, Hoi An, Danang, Hué
—are generally overcrowded, lacking in minimal sanitary
facilities, filthy, evil-smelling and fly-ridden. Crowding is
so extreme that isolation of open wounds from infected
cases is not attempted . . . The patients lie on filthy,
woven straw mats. The odor of garbage, pus and excrement
is omnipresent. . . . We saw flies walking on open wounds
and burns. In Quang Ngai, acute surgical patients are shel-
tered in a garage . . . stagnant, fetid puddles of water pock
the courtyards; and garbage and human excrement foul the
corridors and walkways. . . . Outdated whole blood obtained from U.S. military hospitals is employed for trans-
fusions when available . . . It is not enough to say that hy-
gienic standards in that area are low and that conditions in
Vietnamese hospitals are normative by Asian standards.
There is only one standard to apply: the human standard.
We should be asking, 'What does a human being, gravely
wounded, require to maximize his comfort and chances for
recovery?' To ask less is to adopt a condescension approach-
ing contempt."
A fourth doctor was even more blunt: "As I see it personally," he testified, ". . . it is possible that we have met

1 5 3

the enemy and they are us. . . . I am not sure that some of us [physicians] might not even be half-hearted members of the Viet Cong at the present time as far as that goes."

Once again, Kennedy's response was not the sort of shrieking indignation that could be easily dismissed, and which might also anger Eastland, but measured and painstakingly fair. "Because this effort is unique in our history," Kennedy said at one point, speaking of the American-run programs for assistance for civilian casualties and refugees in Vietnam, "because this approach is by its very nature complex, it is to be expected that deficiencies would result as the delicate balance among competing priorities is affected by time, events and personalities." Nevertheless, he went on to say, "it can be stated without exaggeration that there has been a totally inadequate response by our Government to the needs of the people of South Vietnam—needs that to a large extent have been created by our very presence there. . . ."

Here, then, was effective opposition to the war in a major way. War is hell—everybody knows that; but most people also understand that there are limits. And the evidence that Kennedy's subcommittee was producing demonstrated in the most graphic way that in Vietnam those limits were being ignored and exceeded.

XIII

IN THE MUSEUM
OF PROMISES
UNFULFILLED

WASHINGTON, D.C.—When I sat down with
Kennedy in his Senate office, the first thing I
wanted to find out was what he hoped to accomplish as
whip. At the time he announced his candidacy for the job,
he had said he wanted to use the office to work for "progress and change." And when the Democratic caucus in the
Senate elected him, young Senate liberals like Joseph Tydings of Maryland and Birch Bayh rejoiced, declaring that
with such a nationally prominent figure to lead the charge,
liberals could hope at long last to successfully challenge
the Club's power.

Yet Kennedy and the liberal legion promptly lost their
first contests with the Club. Faced with a steady dwindling
of its number—due mostly to retirement—the Club had

arbitrarily reduced the size of the powerhouse committees to prevent liberals from filling all the vacancies and tipping the balance in their favor. Then, as previously mentioned, the Club brushed aside the seniority system and denied a seat on the all-important Appropriations Committee to Bayh, seating instead the more conservative, and junior, Montoya. Kennedy fought on the losing side of both battles; the question was, how hard?

"It's difficult to categorize my new leadership responsibility," Kennedy answered rather solemnly after taking a series of short puffs on his *cigarillo*. "I start with a feeling that [as whip] I must service all the individual Senators and respect their rights and protect their interests. But I am also aware of the fact that a Senator such as Richard Russell [now deceased, but then chairman of Appropriations] consults with, works with and identifies with a certain group of senators [the Club]. I, as well, will identify myself with a certain group in the Senate; that is, the group dedicated to change and progress and to meeting the needs of the country as I see them."

Senator Russell, of course, had as his base of power the Club's control of the key standing committees—Appropriations, Finance, Armed Services, and Foreign Relations—and also the party organ, the Democratic Steering Committee. Could the liberals develop a base of power too? Kennedy said: "I'd like to see the Democratic Policy Committee, which is made up of progressive and forward-looking senators, fill the function that was originally conceived for it—that is, to formulate ways and means of enacting the party platform into law. As you know, the Policy Committee has not served that function over the past eight years as it should have [it had been the "traffic cop" of the Senate, rather innocuously regulating the flow of legislation to the floor]. But we are now in a new situation with a President of the opposition party. That may invigorate the Policy Committee."

Could the liberals, whether working from the Policy Committee or perhaps some other base of power, buck the seniority system in order to get the Senate moving again? "I have an ambivalence on this," Kennedy replied. "Philosophically, I have reservations about the seniority system. But practically, I can see that in the next ten years it will dramatically alter the Senate. Here, let me show you something."

With this, he got up and disappeared into an adjoining room.

Despite its being bright and airy, the office seemed somber. At either side of the fireplace stood the flags once displayed in John F. Kennedy's office in the White House. The Senator's desk, a modest-sized English antique with a split down the left side, is the one his father used while serving as Ambassador to the Court of St. James during the late thirties, and which President Kennedy later used while serving first in the House, then in the Senate and finally, as President, when it stood in the Fish Room of the White House. Around the walls were photographs of the Kennedy brothers by twos and threes, sailing, campaigning, in academic gowns, laughing, joking, pegging the pigskin. Framed and hung near the door was a letter from John F. Kennedy to his mother, written at about the age of 14 from the Choate School: "Dear Mother, It is the night before exams, so I will write you Wednesday. Lots of love, [scribbled signature] P.S. Can I be godfather to the baby?"

The "baby" returned with a government document in

hand. There was little spring in his step. He seemed for a moment a youthful yet somehow prematurely stooped curator in this museum of bright promises unkept.

Running his finger down a freshly printed list of the members of the standing committees of the Ninety-first Congress, Kennedy stopped at random. "Now these men at the top of the list," he said, "—look at their ages. They're all the same generation. In ten years, through the seniority system, you'll have liberals coming up taking their places. That will be the case with Judiciary, Commerce, Appropriations, Banking and Currency, and others."

Another development of far-reaching significance, Kennedy went on to explain, is that while the South is steadily becoming less "solid" for the Democrats, the Northeast and Midwest are becoming more so. This change, he predicted, will affect the Senate as follows: genuine Republican rivalry and the occasional electoral turnover of Southern seats will lead to a loss of committee seniority for the members from that section of the country, who are invariably conservative, and the concentration of Democratic strength in the Northeast and Midwest will lead to long tenure and increased committee seniority for these members, who tend to be liberal. In the not-too-distant future, therefore, the Senate, which has been in the iron grip of its Southern conservative minority since the election of ex-Senator Warren G. Harding to the Presidency in 1920, is likely to shake off its chains and take up the cudgels for the urban, liberal movement.

But what are Senate liberals to do while waiting for the millennium? Three things, said Kennedy. To begin with, there are already enough liberals and moderates in the Senate today so that if committee assignments could be jockeyed around they might take better advantage of their actual numerical strength. The Club has long used its numbers to maximum advantage and, Kennedy said, he was struck by the fact that in the latest reshuffling of committee assignments, the Southern bloc significantly strengthened its hold over the Judiciary, Finance, and Rules Committees.

The maneuvering was particularly evident in the sudden shift of Robert C. Byrd, the conservative West Virginia Democrat, from Armed Services (which is politically juicy and well-suited to Byrd's proclivities as a hawk) to Judiciary (which is much less rewarding politically yet where the Club's control was slipping due to two retirements) .

"Whether or not they moved into these committees by plan or design, I can't be sure," Kennedy went on to say. "But certainly this is a technique we liberals ought to explore for ourselves. Maybe we could get liberals to give up certain committee assignments even when they have a great interest in a particular committee, when shifting them somewhere else would tip the balance in our favor."

"Another thing for liberals to do," he continued, "is to concentrate on the make-up of the Democratic Steering Committee, to restore some geographical and philosophical balance there. Perhaps the way to go about it is with the Clark resolution to expand its size. Exactly what steps to take to accomplish this are . . . well, I'm just not sure. I think it will take some time to see what will work best to help the liberals gain adequate and equal representation on this key committee."

The third thing Kennedy envisioned for Senate liberals to do was to work within the system as presently constituted, arduous and even humiliating as that may some-times be. For this task, he acknowledged a little obliquely, he is uniquely suited as neither of his brothers were. "There is a tendency," Kennedy said, "to categorize me—usually in contrast to my brothers—as a 'Senate man.' And with some justification. Bob, for example . . ." Kennedy's voice choked and he turned away from me, swallowed hard, then turned back, his eyes glistening with tears, and con-tinued: "Bob had served in a high position in the Admin-istration before he came to the Senate and naturally his interests were broad. President Kennedy had served for a number of years in the House before he came here. For me, however, coming to the Senate at an early age, it has been a place to grow. That meant a period of learning, then chairmanship of a couple of subcommittees last year, still more responsibility this year."

"I have, as everyone does," he continued, "my moments of frustration and anxiety with the legislative process, but, looking at the broad sweep of history and how this insti-tution has been able to deal with the great crises of the past, I have confidence in it. Of course, it failed one time—the Civil War—but I have a healthy appreciation of its ca-pacity to bring about change and human betterment. The Senate may very well be facing its period of greatest chal-lenge right now. Can it be responsive to present needs? I don't know. We'll see. But we have to try."

XIV

KENNEDY, THE MAN;
THE PRESIDENT,
PERHAPS

WASHINGTON, D.C.—Ted Kennedy is a large man. He stands 6'2" in his socks, weighs more than 200 pounds, and, although he is beginning to get just a trifle puffy about the jowls, he has not yet lost his credibility as the first-string Harvard end who scored his team's only touchdown against Yale in 1955.

He is good-looking, too. His smile glitters with a perfect set of teeth and his jaw is broader and more firm than those of his brothers. Frequently, he is dubbed the most handsome Kennedy, although his gentleness and openness seem less fantasy-inspiring to women than the shy, sizzling nature of Bobby.

Before Chappaquiddick, almost anyone who knew Kennedy well would say that his most striking personal quality was his toughness, staunchness and gritty physical courage. After the accident, this view of Kennedy seemed untenable. He was seen as an irresponsible weakling who panicked in a crisis. How is this contradiction to be explained?

Any number of theories are possible. One could say, for example, that the quality of courage was accentuated in Kennedy's character precisely because it was required to hold in check an opposite quality lurking beneath the surface. And that when a particular combination of stresses upset the dynamics of this relationship, the submerged quality—fearfulness, timidity, the tendency to panic—was suddenly released and took possession of him. Whether or not personality can be analyzed in such mechanistic terms, the important point, in my view, is that since there is evidence for contradictory qualities in Kennedy, it must be assumed that *both* aspects of the man really exist rather than that one quality, or set of qualities, is a sham or disguise.

Since so many words have been written about what Chappaquiddick revealed about Kennedy, it would seem worthwhile to set forth some of the evidence of the other side of his personality which has been obsured by negative publicity and which, according to those who have known him for many years, is the side of him that has been almost continuously apparent.

For example, Kennedy's friend, Senator John Tunney, recently recalled with fresh amazement having discovered "the man of steel" in Kennedy one day between classes at the University of Virginia Law School, where they met as fellow students. He and Kennedy were tossing a football back and forth, when Kennedy said he had an idea for something more interesting. "Let's play tackle," said Kennedy. "I'll throw the ball to you and you try to get past me." Tunney, being the son of the boxer Gene Tunney, is no slouch when it comes to competitive sports, yet even he could not quite believe what was coming. Dutifully, he caught the ball when it was tossed and attempted a dash around Kennedy, only to be smeared by 200 pounds of flying meat and gristle pulsing with adrenalin.

"I couldn't *believe* it!" says Tunney. "There we were in our street clothes, with no padding, supposed to be doing full tackles on each other!"

The following summer, when Tunney and Kennedy spent their vacation in Europe and Canada together, Tunney's jaw was to drop again and again. In the South of France, a majestically towering cliff by the sea was, to Kennedy, something to dive from, and on Mont Tremblant in Quebec, the daredevilishly steep Taschereau was something to be *raced* down on skis. If Tunney ever hesitated, Kennedy would goad him on with a Kennedy-family slogan: "When the going gets tough, the tough get going."

Since the plane crash in June, 1964, in which Kennedy suffered a severe spinal injury, he has had to wear a cumbrous plastic back brace, and while he can still sail (his favorite sport) and even play a little tennis and touch football, his dauntless days are behind him. Even so, he is still possessed of instant physical courage. One day not long ago, for example, Kennedy was sailing in a small boat off Bermuda with his old Harvard football teammate Congressman John C. Culver and his wife. The wind was up and they were boiling along. Suddenly—a strong gust, the boat heeled sharply and Culver's wife fell in the water. In a flash, Kennedy went in after her, back brace and all. "He hadn't even a moment's hesitation," Culver recalls. "Just

163

zip! And he was swimming along beside her." It was precisely the reverse of the sort of conduct for which he is remembered at Chappaquiddick, and yet, those who know Kennedy well insist that the way he acted that day off Bermuda is characteristic of him.

Also expressive of Kennedy's inner fiber, they say, is the day-in-day-out courage with which he faces the fact that someday he may present an irresistible target to a psychotic individual disturbed enough to want to try to finish off the last of the Kennedy brothers. Kennedy himself is under no illusions about this possibility. "I know I'm going to get my ass shot off just like Bobby," he once remarked to friends. And yet he persists in public life. Kennedy is, naturally enough, jumpy on occasion. I myself have seen him duck when a car backfires. One day in 1970, when he was attending a centennial celebration of the birth of John Greenleaf Whittier in Haverhill, Massachusetts, someone fired a signal cannon a few dozen feet away from his car just as he was emerging. Kennedy grabbed his stomach and rocked back into the car just as if he had been shot. His face turned white and he was stunned for a few seconds. What seems even more amazing than such episodes as these, however (his friends *do* have a point), is that Kennedy dares to appear in public at all—and ride in motorcades and walk through kitchens shaking hands with dishwashers just as if nothing had ever happened to either of his brothers.

Beyond sheer physical bravery, Kennedy derives strength from his Catholic religion. He has recently been seen attending Mass regularly at the Holy Trinity Church in Georgetown. As frequently as two or three evenings a week, between about 10 and 11 P.M., he drives alone to the Arlington National Cemetery and stands in silence for 20 minutes at his brothers' graves. Kennedy also takes courage from a little blue copy of *Julius Caesar* that he keeps on the desk in his Senate office. He has underlined in red the famous lines with which Caesar rejects the counsel of fear:

> *Cowards die many times before their deaths;*
> *The valiant never taste of death but once.*
> *Of all the wonders that I yet have heard,*
> *It seems to me most strange that men should fear;*
> *Seeing that death, a necessary end,*
> *Will come when it will come.*

Kennedy is often said to be a compulsive politician, obsessed with winning friends and influencing people. This impression—a false one—is largely due to the fact that, as a Kennedy, he was over-written-about, while, being a younger brother in the background, he was not analyzed with any particular care. Whenever his name came up, the work-a-day press simply wheeled out the serviceable Old Quotes about him from family and family friends and let it go at that. He was "the best politician in the family" (J.F.K.) with "the affability of an Irish cop" (Joe, Sr.) who possessed "more moxie than Jack" (Jim Farley).

There is, of course, a degree of truth in the Old Quotes, although they are usually reported straight-facedly with no hint of the fact that when originally uttered they contained a goodly measure of intraclan spoofing. They were not meant to be graven in stone.

But the Old Quotes took on a life of their own, and today the myth of Super-Pol colors virtually everything written or said about Ted Kennedy. Not long ago, for example, a friend of his told a ladies' magazine writer a story about Kennedy's teaching his young son, Teddy, how to shake hands "like a real man." When the story appeared in print, Ted was teaching Teddy how to shake hands "like a politician."

There are other stories about all of Kennedy's intimate friends being politicians, and about their inability, even if their lives depended on it, to discuss anything other than politics for more than two minutes. The stories are not true. Actually, when Kennedy gets together with his close friends, who come from many walks of life, they talk about politics "less than 25 per cent of the time," according to one. What, then, *is* discussed in the main? Well, the sort of things old friends and school chums usually talk about —their families, other friends, child rearing, their hopes, life, fate, music, the world, the Federalist Papers, pollution, travel, sailing, the fine points of good cheese cake.

Kennedy is also a conscientious family man. Whenever possible, he takes with him on his peregrinations between Boston, Hyannis Port, Washington and Palm Beach the whole gang—his wife Joan and their three children, Kara, 12; Teddy, 11; and Patrick, $4\frac{1}{2}$—in order to spend all the time he can in their company. In fact, wherever Kennedy may be, he invariably telephones his children once a day. Young Teddy, especially, has become obsessed with the thought that his father will be killed just as his uncles have been, and so Kennedy reassures him every day with a telephone call. Kennedy is also remarkably good about remembering all 16 of the birthdays of his and his brothers' children, and he even makes a point of catching the tail end of each of their almost-continuous stream of birthday parties. Last year at Halloween, he surprised his neighbors by dressing up in a sheet and accompanying the children on their trick-or-treat rounds.

Joan Kennedy is a radiant blonde who was once chosen queen of the Floral Pageant in Bermuda. More recently she has attracted attention with her stylish and daring mini-skirts and plunging necklines. All of which creates a not-very-accurate picture of her in the press. She is really a quite shy and warm person.

An accomplished pianist, Joan majored in music at Manhattanville College of the Sacred Heart in Purchase, New York, and a few years ago she won critical praise for an appearance with the Washington National Symphony as narrator for Prokofiev's "Peter and the Wolf." Concert-going is the family's chief cultural interest, although Ted really prefers Engelbert Humperdinck to Paul Hindemith and Dionne Warwick to Richard Wagner.

All this is not to suggest that Kennedy is not consumed with politics a great deal of the time, nor to deny that he is uncommonly good at it—an intuitive politician, in fact. "He has a remarkable ability to press his point without arousing the opposition," says one Senate colleague. "The South, for example, loves him. And he's not buying their respect through surrender. Birch Bayh and Phil Hart say he's the toughest member on Judiciary."

Southerners, including those who fought him tooth and nail when Kennedy ran for whip, do not dispute this sentiment. "I don't think the whip fight left any scars," says one.

"And Kennedy knows how to use that little black box," says another Senator, pointing to his telephone. "When he was running for whip and needed my vote, he happened to call when I wasn't home. My wife answered. He didn't just exchange a few pleasantries and then ask when to call back. He stayed on the phone for at least five minutes, and—Jeez!—when I got home if I'd told my wife I wasn't going to vote for Kennedy I'd have been sleeping out in the backyard."

Another side of the myth is Kennedy's reputation as a wit. Almost every popular public figure these days is alleged to be clever—the mass media, the temper of the times demand it—but, because of the genuine wit of Kennedy's older brothers, he, especially, is believed to have the makings of a writer for "Laugh-In." Several of his Senate colleagues, for example, insist that he is one of the most amusing chaps they have met in a long while, but when pressed for a concrete example of his humorousness they scratch their heads in dismay.

The explanation turns out to be twofold. In the first place, Kennedy is a gifted impersonator. He used to be able to make his brothers double up with laughter with his imitations of their grandfather, Honey Fitz, and of Jimmy Manchin, a likeable, earnest West Virginian who travelled around his state introducing the Kennedys in the state primary campaign of 1960. It would take an equally gifted impersonator to recreate any of this orally, and consequently most of it is lost as soon as delivered.

In the second place, Kennedy does not possess the ironic, literary and highly quotable wit of President Kennedy, nor the biting sarcasm of Bobby, which was also repeatable and printable. Ted Kennedy is, instead, a genial ribber.

"Hey! There he is. The great man from the North End!" Kennedy will sing out when greeting a Boston politician. Seeing a colleague duck out of the Old Senate Office Building in mid-afternoon: "Leavin' early today, Senator?

M'gosh, the farmers back home are still workin'." Catching the same member departing early again: "Ah, this isn't a bank, ya know."

Kennedy is also something of a prankster. One of the running gags in his Senate office is that when a staff member goofs, Kennedy used to snatch off the goofer's "PT-109" or "Kennedy-62" tie clasp (souvenirs of various Kennedy campaigns), saying with mock sternness: "And you're not gettin' this back, either!" Frequently, Kennedy kept his word and so today staff members rarely wear tie clasps.

Even Bobby's death did not completely subdue the prankster in him. One day, just a few weeks after the assassination, Kennedy invited a couple of his Senate staff members up to Hyannis Port and took them sailing on the *Victura,* Jack Kennedy's old racing sloop. It was a choppy day. David Burke was sitting on the bow with his back to the waves facing Kennedy, who was at the tiller. The conversation concerned the Presidential campaign and it was being carried on at a fairly serious level. Then, in a very quiet voice, Kennedy said: "Are you ready, Dave?" Before Burke could answer he was engulfed by a huge wave that sent him sprawling across the deck. Kennedy had seen a big one coming and deliberately plowed right into it. Much hilarity followed, and the three sailors came home drenched but laughing.

A favorite after-dinner Kennedy game, played only with close friends, is the offering of "funny toasts." Kennedy's old Harvard friend, John Culver, for instance, is occasionally toasted for his exemplary generosity—the principal illustration of which is the time Culver greedily swilled down an entire thermos of fish chowder that was intended for a group of four who were crewing for Kennedy in the

Nantucket Regatta. John Tunney is frequently lauded for having learned "that most important lesson in life—that a man should run for office without any help from his family." Tunney then roars with laughter because he knows what's coming—a reference to the fact that midway through his first campaign he had taken a poll, found himself behind and instantly called in Gene Tunney and Jack Dempsey to help out with "a little family identification."

Kennedy usually laughs, too. And he laughs loud. "I can hear him laugh," says Senator George McGovern whose office is across a courtyard about half a block away from Kennedy's. "It's loud, and it's a laugh of joy. It's the kind of laugh that makes you feel better about life."

Kennedy is noted around the Senate for his warmth and thoughtfulness. These qualities are no myth. One day in 1967, when he walked into the Senate chamber and found on his desk the report of the Ethics Committee recommending the censure of Senator Thomas J. Dodd of Connecticut, he put down his papers and walked directly to Dodd's office. There was no duplicity involved in the fact that he knew he was going to vote in favor of the motion to censure; he only wished to extend his sympathy, and to ask if he could place any personal resource at Dodd's disposal. Kennedy was the only Senator to visit Dodd that day.

On another occasion, very shortly after the death of Robert Kennedy, he learned that the daughter of one of his colleagues had been arrested on a possession of marijuana charge. "Ted was the first one to call," this Senator says. "He just wanted to know if there was anything he could do. It struck me as such a decent thing—to call at a time when he was so deep in his own grief."

"There's no calculation about the way he acts," says another of Kennedy's friends. "He's just that way. He's the most thoughtful man I know."

Thoughtfulness in this sense, of course, has nothing to do with intellectual acuity. In this respect, Ted Kennedy does not seem to invite comparison with his brothers. He does not display the piercing intellect, or flair for succinct summary, for which President Kennedy was noted; he impresses people, rather, as shrewd and sound and as a hard worker—a plugger. He reads thought-provoking books, but he does not read rapidly. Indeed, I have personally observed on several occasions that he moves his lips when he reads—the mark of a painfully slow reader. Nor is Ted much of a writer. One speechwriter with whom he has worked closely over the years comments, "Ted had a great deal of difficulty with syntax when he began in politics and, while he is improving, he still tends to surround a problem with words."

And Ted Kennedy is much less sure of himself intellectually than were either of his brothers. In the preparation of a speech, for example, President Kennedy used to start by briefing his writers, the writers would take notes, and then they would come back with a draft for discussion. Ted Kennedy, on the other hand, usually has the writer complete a draft first and *then* enters into a discussion, in the course of which he is unusually receptive to other people's suggestions.

So dependent is he on his speechwriters, in fact, that he even assigned a group of them the task of writing the famous eulogy he delivered for Bobby at Saint Patrick's Cathedral. "We felt pretty funny about it," one of the writers told me, "because how could *we* know what he felt about his brother? He just said write something on the theme of love. Some of the guys wrote polemics, and some borrowed from *The Founding Father* [a biography of the late Joseph P. Kennedy]. I wrote what turned out to be the start and finish of the speech he finally delivered, but I've always felt odd about it. I thought maybe that was the one speech he shouldn't have asked us to write."

If Kennedy seems overly dependent on his "brain trust," however, he is not unique among politicians in this respect. Most men in public life are not profound thinkers, nor are they literary artists (Lincoln, Wilson, Franklin Roosevelt, and John F. Kennedy were striking exceptions). Politicians almost always depend on the idea men and speechwriters they surround themselves with; furthermore they usually think in terms of the spoken as opposed to the written word, invariably preferring a good oral briefing to even a brilliantly written memo. Politicians are performers, too, exercising leadership rather than intellectual qualities, and having talents for dramatization rather than conceptualization.

Judged by this standard, Ted Kennedy is the equal if not the superior of his brothers. In fact, his gift as an impersonator and a raconteur was the chief thing he had over his older brothers, who used to listen to him take off others or tell a tall tale with delight—and envy. Today, Kennedy has the ability to take a speech text and "make it live and breathe," as one of his admiring colleagues in the Senate expresses it, and he is probably one of the two or three best public speakers in the Senate. Because of his gift for interpretive reading he has been invited on a number of occasions to narrate Aaron Copland's "Lincoln Portrait" to the accompaniment of the Boston Symphony Orchestra. He reads this text with power and dignity.

On the public platform, at impromptu press conferences

and at receptions, Kennedy is also uncommonly effective. He appears well informed on the issues; handles questions graciously and, when the occasion requires, sharply; is almost never rattled, and comes across as solid, confident and committed, whether or not one agrees with his point of view. I recall, for example, seeing Kennedy and Mayor John V. Lindsay together at a reception in New York City in late 1971. Both men made short, off-the-cuff speeches and cracked a few jokes. Beside Kennedy, Lindsay seemed a lightweight. I kept thinking that Lindsay was coming off as awkward, a tyro dabbling in national politics, whereas Kennedy appeared the compleat pro, perfectly at ease practicing the family business.

Kennedy also radiates that infectious and indefinable thing the professionals call "star quality." His physical presence turns heads. There is something about him that seems *interesting,* something about him at which one wants to get a closer look. Kennedy understands this, and prudently underplays his glamor. The glittering smile is always a little restrained, the boyish enthusiasm kept under tight control. One does not get too much of it that way, nor does one think of him as flip or silly.

Kennedy possesses a final strength. An old friend of his expresses it this way: "Today, Ted enjoys a political sophistication that is far beyond his years. It's there because of all those who went before. This was the case with each of his brothers, too. Joe, Jr. learned from his father. Jack benefited from his father and from Joe. Each in his turn benefited from all of his predecessors. And in the most substantive way. Now, all those who have gone before have a cumulative effect that is evident in Ted. He is the inheritor of the private family experience of all the Kennedys."

This last statement touches on what is Edward Ken-

1 7 3

nedy's perhaps most formidable asset. Throughout his adult life, but particularly during the ten-year period starting in 1958, when he managed John Kennedy's campaign for the Senate, and ending in 1968, when he served as a manager of Bobby Kennedy's Presidential campaign, he was a top lieutenant of the Kennedy organization and privy to the innermost councils of this remarkable family in its adventure at the heights of American politics. The Kennedy organization was by no means all-powerful, nor were the decisions of its councils all-wise. His brothers were not even always successful—as in the Bay of Pigs, or in the Oregon primary. Yet the Kennedys were graced with a large share of prudence, success and power, and were extraordinarily placed during an era of grave crisis and change. All that cannot but have had the most profound effect on the last of the Kennedys.

As time goes by, his recollection of all the events of his brothers' ascendancy, of who said what to whom, which factors were taken into account, what decisions made, may blur. Doubtless, there will be times when he may feel he would give anything he owns for two minutes of counsel with Jack or Bob. And there will be enchanters who seem to fill this void by insisting that they know how one or the other of his brothers would have reacted in a given situation. And moments of trial in which Ted Kennedy will think he sees the face of Jack when it is only mist, or hears the voice of Bobby when it is just the wind in the rigging.

Nevertheless, what he carries with him that the crimes of Dallas and Los Angeles cannot take away is that special Kennedy amalgam of liberalism and sophistication, steadiness and attack, which were both bred and drummed into his sinews. That may be less than legend has made it seem, but it is still much to contend with.

INDEX